THE BLACK POPLAR

The Black Poplar

History, Ecology and Conservation

Fiona Cooper

'The Poplars gratify three of our senses. They are pleasing to the sight, their leaves make an agreeable rustling sound, and the resinous buds of some species diffuse a delicious aroma'

H. Gilbert-Carter (1936) *British Trees and Shrubs,*
Oxford, Clarendon Press.

WINDgather
PRESS

The Black Poplar: History, Ecology and Conservation

Published by: Windgather Press Ltd, 29 Bishop Road, Bollington, Macclesfield, Cheshire SK10 5NX

Distributed by: Central Books Ltd, 99 Wallis Road, London E9 5LN

British Library Cataloguing-in-Publication Data
A catalogue record for this book is available from the British Library

ISBN 1–905119–05–4

Designed, typeset and originated by Carnegie Publishing Ltd, Chatsworth Road, Lancaster

Printed and bound by CPI Bath Press

Contents

List of Figures

For Mike

Acknowledgements

Firstly, I would like to thank you, the reader, for buying this book, and hope that you will find it enjoyable, inspirational and informative. A huge debt of gratitude is owed to a large number of people for making it possible. Marianne Jones, of the Environment Agency, was the initial catalyst for my enthusiasm, and set me off on the long road which led to this book. Everyone involved in my Ph.D. study at the University of Nottingham, my supervisors Prof Charles Watkins and Dr Zoe Wilson, and various friends and colleagues in the School of Geography and School of Biological Sciences, including Kirsty Jewell, Emel Okan, Emel Sozen, Rosalba and Heriberto Gomez, Georgina Endfield and Cai Yun Yang, provided advice and support. During my writing up period, my friends Tracy Purslow and Ade Sarwycz insisted upon daily updates on the amount of work I had produced in the preceding 24 hours, something that kept me strongly motivated, and was more help than they could have imagined. An enormous number of people helped me during fieldwork, by accompanying me, letting me stay and generally smoothing the way with landowners where necessary; their names are listed below and I would like them to know how much their help was appreciated. Many people and organisations (too numerous to mention) have very kindly sent me records of black poplars and without this information my distribution data would have been nowhere near as comprehensive as it currently stands.

I am grateful to all who encouraged me to go ahead with this book, and to those who have helped with recent research: Bill Reynolds, for his wealth of information on the Botloe's Green tree; Paul Hand, for valuable information on the Arbor Tree and for introducing me to the Hanging Tree; Michael Roberts, for showing me the River Shannon population; and Desmond Hobson, for enormous amounts of information about all sorts of populations. Desmond, together with Annette Harley (Edgar Milne-Redhead's daughter) also very kindly gave me additional information about Edgar's life and work. Dr Richard Mabey gave me information on the Vale of Aylesbury population. Joe Walsh, Arboricultural Officer for Manchester Leisure, first alerted me to the problem of *Venturia populina* and provided me with a great deal of historical information; he is generally a mine of information. Very grateful thanks also go to: Rosie Evans of Beambridge, Aston on Clun, who gave me pictures of the Arbor Tree; to Michael Tennyson for permission to use the drawing of Cholstrey Barn; to Dave Phillips for various professional pictures throughout the book; and to John White for the pictures of turned bowls. John and the

Forestry Commission kindly allowed me to use their catkins illustrations. Thanks are also due to Scenesetters, of Bucknell in Shropshire, who constructed the maps from my distribution data. Alan Holmes very kindly gave up a day of his time to drive me around the Vale of Aylesbury, and also checked information in the local libraries for me. I would also like to thank: Ken Adams; Frances Claxton; Arthur Chater; Kirsty Creighton, Carey and Peter Ennis; Steven Falk; Sir Richard Hanbury-Tenison; Desmond Hobson; Alan Holmes; Trevor James; Peter Jepson; Marianne Jones; Norman Lewis; Ian Morgan; John Parker; my father, Richard Phillips; Kevin Pyne; John Richfield; Michael Roberts; Eric Rogers; Gwen Rogers; Val and Barry Shimmield; and Brian Thornton. I am grateful to the many other people who have given me information but, of course, any errors, misinterpretations and omissions are entirely my own.

I must thank my cats (Barnum and Sweep, both of whom are, very sadly, no longer with us, and Cobweb, Merlin, Jacob, Crawford and Pepper) for their company during the long hours of data analysis, word processing and editing, although I could have done without paws on the keyboard, which frequently led to some unusual characters within the text!

Thanks are due to my publisher, Richard Purslow, for being so enthusiastic about my work, and extremely patient in seeing the project through to its logical conclusion.

Lastly, but by no means least, I would like to thank my husband, Mike, for financial support, help with domestic duties, endless patience and moral support, particularly during my Ph.D., but also in the time spent preparing the manuscript for this book.

Preface

In February 1996, whilst studying as an undergraduate, I received a telephone call from Marianne Jones of the Environment Agency (then Marianne Le Ray), for whom I had been lucky enough to work during the previous summer vacation. She asked me if I would be interested in some Easter vacation work involving data collation for a black poplar project in the Shropshire, Montgomeryshire and Worcestershire area. I was delighted to be asked, and readily agreed to help in any way I could. I then realised that, although I had heard of black poplars, I wasn't sure whether I had actually seen one! Marianne warned me at the outset that I would either become obsessed with the species, or simply regard it as just another tree. This book is testament to the fact that I fell victim to an obsession: thank you, Marianne; black poplar has given me some wonderful experiences, led me to places I would not have otherwise visited and to meet people I would not otherwise have met. Not least, it led me to undertake a Ph.D. (researching the geographic distribution and genetic diversity of black poplar), something that, ten years ago, starting out as a mature student, I would have thought to be an impossible undertaking.

This book tells the story of black poplar throughout history: its place in the landscape, its timber and medicinal uses, its decline in popularity, and its resurgence since the early 1970s, as a result of Edgar Milne-Redhead's enthusiasm and dedicated work in bringing its plight to public notice. It also looks at the ways in which genetic analysis has been used to investigate levels of genetic diversity in order to conserve the tree and ensure that it is not lost from our landscape. The book is necessarily broad-based in its subject matter, covering all aspects of research from folklore to genetics; as with the yew (though less well-known than that ancient species), black poplar occupies an important place in many aspects of British culture. In addition, I felt it necessary to include a section on conservation, planting and management; black poplar has survived for the past 300 years solely as a result of efforts by humans in planting the tree in hedgerows, and its survival is unlikely to continue without considerable human assistance in future centuries. A great deal of attention has been given to the so-called Manchester poplar, widely planted throughout the North West, and whilst the population is arguably of lesser aesthetic and ecological importance, it is a vital piece of industrial and social history. It is about to be lost from the Manchester landscape, and in writing this book I was adamant that its history and subsequent loss be adequately recorded for future generations. The other major population in Britain is that found in the Vale of Aylesbury, again a planted population. There are approximately 4,000 to 5,000 trees in the vale, and they must have had considerable importance as timber trees in previous times, although little documentary evidence exists to support this hypothesis.

Another peculiarity of black poplar is that it is not a woodland tree, and most naturalists and authors associate trees with woodland; lone trees that do not form part of woodland are less well understood, and perhaps under-represented in the literature. Therefore, I hope that the publication of this book is timely, and that it will bring together the many groups actively involved in the conservation of black poplar throughout Britain.

Finally – and this is most important – I hope that I will have succeeded in transmitting some of my enthusiasm for this magnificent, charismatic tree through these pages to the reader, and will have encouraged future generations to share my appreciation of black poplar.

Dr Fiona Cooper
Church Stretton, 2005

CHAPTER ONE

Cultural and Botanical Features of the Black Poplar

Introduction

With its dramatic silhouette, black poplar (*Populus nigra* subsp *betulifolia)* is one of Britain's largest, most magnificent and charismatic trees. Over some four centuries, it has inspired silviculturists, tree enthusiasts, artists and writers, such as John Evelyn, John Constable, William Cowper and Gerard Manley Hopkins. Curiously, John Clare did not mention it, possibly because of its rarity in Northamptonshire, where he gained his knowledge and inspiration. It is also one of our most rare and endangered trees, for reasons that will be discussed in detail in later chapters.

The tree is capable of growing to around 40 metres, and is characterised by an extremely distinctive, untidy silhouette, with down-sweeping lower branches and, often, a heavy lean. As a lone tree it has enormous landscape impact, which can be seen in the stunning tree on the banks of the River Severn near Bewdley in Worcestershire (Figure 1), a tree I have visited on many occasions, for no other reason than to admire its magnificence and dominance of its surroundings, undiminished even when a steam train is passing behind on the Severn Valley Railway. Such is its presence in the landscape, it is difficult to imagine how botanists could have mistaken it for its close relation, the comparatively dull hybrid, *Populus x canadensis* (Figure 2); there has been considerable confusion between the two species in the past, leading to a great deal of over-recording of black poplar. Thanks largely to the work of one man, Edgar Milne-Redhead, who received an MBE in 1996 on his 90th birthday in recognition of his black poplar conservation work, the tree was brought to public attention and today enjoys a greater level of popularity and interest than ever before. It should therefore be brought back from the brink of extinction.

The culture and botany of black poplar has to be seen in the context of changing perceptions of trees and woodland over time, explored briefly below. Trees have been an emotive issue for centuries, but perhaps more so in recent years, since forest destruction has moved to the forefront of conservation issues. I have also given a very brief history of the changes to our landscape during the past 6,000 years, before moving on to discuss black poplar in general terms.

FIGURE 1.
A magnificent example of a lone black poplar in its native floodplain habitat; the tree is adjacent to the River Severn near Bewdley in Worcestershire.
DAVE PHILLIPS

FIGURE 2.
A hybrid poplar; this example no longer exists due to wind-throw. Although the tree displays arching branches characteristic of black poplar, it lacks the deeply fissured bark and the vivid green of the native species.
MARIANNE JONES

Shifting perception of trees and woodland

Trees and woodlands have been the subject of changing human attitudes throughout history and prehistory. Wilderness and woodland, which covered the landscape until around 6,000 years ago, were largely perceived to be fearsome and dangerous places,[1] whilst in the early seventeenth century, when the ideology of conquering, controlling and perfecting nature was prevalent, a survivor of natural woodland was sadly known as a 'weed tree', rather than as an important component of the landscape and an object of beauty in its own right. Formal landscapes were favoured around this period. However, in the late seventeenth century, a shift in stance towards the natural world began to take place, and by the end of the eighteenth century, landscapes that were wild and apparently uncultivated, rather than regular and uniform, were fashionable; Humphry Repton, the influential landscape designer and author, suggested that straight fences and pollarded trees were 'objects of profit not beauty'.[2]

Arboreal change in Britain

Primitive agriculture commenced in the Mesolithic period (6,000–4,500 BP) and accelerated during the Neolithic period (4,500–2,000 BP),[3] resulting in large-scale forest clearance to make way for crop production; tree removal has been a steady, almost continual process since Mesolithic times, although, arguably, it has declined in the last 2,000 years. Tree planting has undergone periods of popularity over the past three centuries or so, as, for example, when parkland was in fashion during the eighteenth and nineteenth centuries, and, more recently, in the late twentieth century, as a result of concern over large-scale deforestation. By the beginning of the twentieth century, only 4 per cent of the UK consisted of woodland[4] and, between 1950 and 1975, some 50 million trees were lost from the British Isles, almost half of which losses were due to drought and disease.[5] Vast tracts of land were utilised by the Forestry Commission for softwood plantations, such as *Picea sichensis* (Sitka spruce), although such plantations have been held in low regard by conservationists. In 1978, following the mid twentieth-century tree losses, Dutch elm disease devastated the population of elm in Britain (numbering approximately 25 million trees). In order to reverse the trend of tree losses, the Department of the Environment initiated a successful campaign to 'Plant a Tree in '73', which resulted in the formation of the Tree Council in 1974. As well as raising general public awareness, the Council organises the annual National Tree Week each November. Awareness of the tree loss issue was further raised by widespread press reports about rainforest destruction in the 1980s and in more recent times, attitudes have been changed by articles in the written media and on the television, where numerous nature programmes have 'awakened great appreciation of our natural riches'.[6] As Hayman says, 'we never tire of expressing our love of trees, of recalling how refreshed and inspired we feel in their presence'.[7]

There are several theories about the current popularity of tree planting. The tree can be regarded as a hegemony, because of the size of the organism.[8] We regard them as special because they are bigger than us, 'both physically and metaphorically',[9] and they are comparatively enduring; the lifespan of a tree can be thousands of years (dependent upon species). Perhaps they are the antithesis of mortality; as Schama suggests, 'groves of trees' are 'fitting décor for our earthy remains'.[10] Trees and forests are particularly rich sources for environmental disputes, and give an important insight into the relationship between society and nature. They are a 'battleground for industry, governments, and conservation organisations, and give rise to an array of positions that are represented in the conflicts that ensue'. Thomas suggests that various interested groups use tree-planting to 'bolster an image of environmental stewardship';[11] their size gives them the greatest visual impact of any plant, and as long-lived organisms they are therefore excellent objects for environmental campaigns. Cohen also discusses the removal of status between the *produced* and the *natural* tree, suggesting that 'the tree in the garden is in reality no less other, no less worthy of our wonder and respect, than the tree in an ancient forest that has never known an axe or saw'; this point would perhaps be an excellent topic for debate between ecologists and horticulturists.[12] Cohen's views on planted trees are particularly relevant to the status of black poplar in the UK, since the majority of the remaining trees, particularly in hedgerows, were planted.

The legal framework for tree conservation

Despite popular belief, trees have very little legal protection. In the United Kingdom and the Republic of Ireland local authorities may use Tree Preservation Orders (TPO) to protect single specimens, lines or groups of trees and woodland.[13] TPOs were introduced by the Town and Country Planning Act 1947, and prohibit the cutting down, topping, lopping or wilful destruction of a tree on which an order has been placed without the consent of the local authority involved. Three criteria have to be fulfilled for a tree to become the subject of a TPO; a tree or trees have to be at risk from development; to be under threat from felling; and to have amenity value. However, TPOs have been known to work against preservation and to have a negative effect. Where TPOs are placed on woodlands, owners may feel that no management can take place, and woodland can therefore become derelict; it was estimated that, in 1964, 23,000 ha of woodland was affected in this way.[14] In a more recent instance, a black poplar in Worcestershire (Figure 3), which was the subject of a TPO, was in danger of causing damage to an adjacent property by falling branches. In order to preserve the tree, the landowner was prepared to pay for tree surgery to reduce it to a height where its branches would no longer be a danger. However, due to a lack of understanding by planners, the tree officer from the local council insisted the tree be reduced to 0.6 m in height, which has effectively destroyed it entirely.[15]

FIGURE 3.
A neglected old pollard at Cutnall Green, near Droitwich in Worcestershire. This tree was the subject of a Tree Preservation Order, which, rather than protecting it, sadly resulted in its destruction.
DAVE PHILLIPS

FIGURE 4.
A lovely mature female black poplar (white fluff can be seen in the crown of the tree), that stands at Grimley in Worcestershire.
DAVE PHILLIPS

The current popularity of black poplar

As Rackham rightly states, 'no other native tree can compare with [black poplar] in rugged grandeur' and 'more than almost any other tree, [it] reminds us of the splendour of the medieval countryside'.[16] It is a delight to chance upon a mature specimen, particularly when it is growing in what is regarded as its native lowland floodplain habitat. Although the species has been identified as one of Britain's most endangered native trees,[17] it is currently enjoying a high level of popularity, with various conservation projects ensuring its continuing place in the British landscape. A number of groups and individuals throughout the country, such as wildlife trusts and county councils, together with local *ad hoc* conservation groups, are establishing black poplar stool beds and carrying out planting programmes.

The biological and botanical features of black poplar, coupled with its rarity and place in history and folklore, make it one of Britain's most fascinating trees to study, whether that be in the field, in the laboratory or from the comfort of an armchair. It is a notoriously difficult tree to identify, with a number of inter-relating characteristics that all need to be taken into account.

The botanical features of black poplar

The optimum time for identification is in late May, June or early July. Firstly, one needs to stand back and look at the overall 'jizz' of the tree; if the tree is standard (Figure 4) and has not been pollarded – a pollard is a tree that has been cut at between two and four metres above ground level, and then allowed to grow again to produce a crop of branches (Figure 5) – it should have an untidy, spreading habit. It can grow as tall as 40 metres in height, with down-sweeping lower branches and up-sweeping upper branches (Figure 6). The bark should be dark grey-brown, deeply and irregularly fissured, with bosses and burrs, and the leaf colour should be a vivid green (as opposed to the duller green of the hybrid). Looking more closely at the tree, the tips of the twigs are ascending and the current years' growth is ochre coloured, often with a yellow, viscous exudate; twigs are cylindrical (terete) in shape. Buds are outward turning, with a ginger, shellac appearance. Black poplar leaves display great variability, both within and between individual trees; generally they are deltoid-ovate in shape, with laterally compressed, pubescent (hairy) petioles and serrated, but not hooked, margins. The aphid *Pemphigus populitransversus*, which causes spiral galls, frequently deforms leaf petioles. Leaf glands are absent from the junction of the petiole with the leaf blade.

Native black poplar does not support mistletoe; despite this, what appears from morphological characteristics to be a genuine black poplar near Craven Arms in Shropshire has a mistletoe bough amongst its branches. However, a genetic study in 1999 suggested that this tree differed in its genetic makeup from other individuals in the study,[18] indicating that the tree was not pure black poplar, and had probably undergone genetic 'pollution'. As with the holly and the yew, the tree is dioecious, in that male and female catkins feature on separate trees; this is evident in late March or early April when the tree is in flower, prior to leaf flush. Male catkins are deep crimson; female catkins are bright green. When seed is shed in June, female trees are surrounded by copious amounts of hydrophobic 'fluff', which surrounds the seed, giving the appearance of a layer of snow.

Many black poplars in Britain are pollards; they are generally some two to three metres in height, and the amount of crown growth is dependent upon when they were last pollarded. As with standards, leaf size and shape can vary greatly; newly trimmed individuals display atypical leaf characteristics, in that they tend to produce small, diamond shaped leaves, or alternatively, large, misshapen leaves, and are therefore unreliable in terms of identification.

Unfortunately, there are a number of contradictory factors that can cause confusion when endeavouring to identify a black poplar. Trees may vary from the description given above in several ways. It is possible to find both pubescent (hairy) and glabrous (smooth) twigs on the same tree;[19] some trees do not display bossing habit;[20] bark colour may vary between geographical areas;[21] and variation may occur in the shape of leaves, both on individual trees and between different specimens.[22] Outside the optimum identification time, other problems may present themselves. Leaf glands, which are usually absent, may appear in late summer,[23] and in many trees, pubescence disappears in mid-July.[24] A full list of identification characteristics for use in the field can be found in Appendix A (below).

Habitat and natural sites

The original habitat of the tree is the subject of much debate. It is believed by some workers to be a component of floodplain forest,[25] but Rackham and White (unpublished) do not regard black poplar to be a woodland tree.[26] Following this theory, its numbers would have been expected to increase following clearance of floodplain forest by Neolithic peoples, as it would have colonised neglected wet areas.[27] Ellenberg considered black poplar a pioneer species of floodplain forest in Europe, which matured into mixed broad-leaved forests, consisting of *Ulmus, Quercus, Fraxinus, Salix* and *Alnus.*[28] In British floodplains, *Betula* could be added to this group.[29] An argument in favour of black poplar's place in floodplain forest is the presence of its European counterpart in the fragmentary floodplain forest on the River Drome[30] (Figure 7) and the River Loire in France (personal observation). However, its appearance would have been very different from the isolated individuals seen today. As a heliophilous species, it requires light and space; competition from other species prevents it from developing its characteristic silhouette. I have seen trees in woodland near Abergavenny, and in floodplain forest on the River Loire near Angers in France, all of which lacked the characteristics of the more isolated individuals.

Opinions as to the optimum conditions for the tree vary somewhat. Tansley

FIGURE 5.
Newly pollarded tree in a garden hedgerow at Moseley, near Worcester. The tree is displaying the vigorous growth so typical of trees having recently undergone surgery.
PETER NORMAN

FIGURE 6.
Skyward view of a standard tree, illustrating the arching branches, which are so characteristic of mature standard trees.
PETER NORMAN

mentioned black poplar as being rare in oakwood, but occasionally found in marsh wood.[31] Peterken believes that 'hedgerows and riverside fringes containing black poplar' ... 'can be regarded as fragments of the floodplain forest of major lowland rivers of Britain'.[32] Bean suggests that 'it is a mistaken belief that poplar thrives on wet soil',[33] and a study by Van Splunder *et al.* suggests that black poplar is drought tolerant.[34] I have, in fact, seen trees thriving at varying altitudes throughout the species' range. The famous diarist, Evelyn, regarded poplar as an 'aquatical' species,[35] whilst Cook refers to the tree as the 'water poplar' and states that it 'loves to grow by riversides, or in ground that is wet, or such as holds water much'.[36] Gilbert-Carter regarded it as 'not uncommon on rich wet soils in southern and eastern England'.[37]

These references generally support the theory of black poplar being a wetland tree, with the exception of Bean, who may have been correct in referring to it not always being found in lowland floodplain; there are many planted examples which can be found at altitudes as high as approximately 300 m.

The evolution and distribution of black poplar

Black poplar 'in the aggregate sense',[38] as opposed to the many hybrids and subspecies, which are found in more closely defined areas, has a broad distribution: from Britain in the west to central China in the north and east; and from north Africa and Iran in the south to north-west India and Afghanistan in the south-east.[39] Black poplar belongs to the Angiospermidae (flowering plants) class of plants, which arose during the Lower Cretaceous period, between 141 and 100 million years ago. Wind-pollinated dicotyledoneous angiosperms arose during the Upper Cretaceous, commencing some 90 million years ago, and fossil leaves resembling modern *Populus* genera have been commonly found in North America, Europe and Asia.[40] Fossilised poplar pollen has been identified in rocks from the Cretaceous age, although this pollen was thought to be from aspen,[41] but as the two are virtually impossible to distinguish, the sample may or may not include black poplar. Godwin records poplar or willow charcoal from Bronze Age sites in *History of the British Flora*, but does not specify the poplar pollen as originating from black poplar,[42] suggesting that he was uncertain of the status of the latter species in the British Isles.

In Britain, *P. nigra* subsp *betulifolia* is found largely south of an imaginary line between the Lune and Humber estuaries, although isolated examples can be found further north; large populations can be found in Lancashire, Manchester, the Welsh border, East Anglia and Buckinghamshire, particularly in the Vale of Aylesbury.

The classification of *Populus* genus

The Salicaceae family contains the genera *Populus* (poplars) and *Salix* (willows). The genus is divided into five sections and approximately thirty species, dependent upon the authority consulted. Elwes and Henry suggest twenty-five species and five sections,[43] whilst Laidlaw suggests nearly forty, in five sections, although he includes black poplar hybrids in this figure.[44] Gilbert-Carter suggests twenty to thirty species in three sections: Leuce, Aegirus and Tacamahaca. The same author also mentions a third genus, *Chosenia*, found in the far east of the range, describing it as an intermediate between *Populus* and *Salix*.[45] It is possible that confusion regarding numbers of species has arisen as a result of great uncertainty over both the scientific and common nomenclature of poplar, which has resulted in several names for one species or clone.

P. nigra subsp *betulifolia* was not recognised as a distinct sub-species by early European botanists.[46] This recognition did not come until the tree was exported to America and found there by Michaux in the early nineteenth century, growing by the Hudson River, and named *P. hudsonica* Michx.[47] The same species was named *P. betulifolius* Pursh by the German botanist, Frederick Pursh.[48] This sub-species is thought to differ from that found in mainland Europe, *P. nigra* subsp *nigra* (other than on the extreme western fringe of Europe, where the black poplar found in Britain grows), only by an absence of pubescence on shoots and petioles. However, further work needs to be conducted on morphological differences between the two sub-species[49] and, furthermore, it is not known whether the two sub-species are genetically distinct.

Augustus Henry and G. S. Cansdale carried out extensive work to clarify *Populus* taxonomy.[50] However, a certain amount of confusion still exists today. Whilst two distinct sub-species are currently accepted, one found in Britain and the other in Europe, Gilbert-Carter describes three: 'Var. *genuina* (rare): young twigs and petioles glabrous, leaves triangular-ovate, base cuneate; var. *viridis:* young twigs and petioles hairy, leaves triangular-ovate, base truncate; var *betulifolia:* young twigs and petioles hairy, leaves rhomboid, base cuneate, apex long acuminate'. Var. *genuina*, which Gilbert-Carter describes as rare, is probably the hairless sub-species found in mainland Europe.[51]

The Lombardy poplar

It is perhaps important to mention the well-known Lombardy poplar at this stage, as this form is familiar to many people, having been widely planted throughout Britain and Europe as a shelterbelt or amenity species. The leaves and twigs of Lombardy poplar are almost identical to native black poplar, making identification without a tree description and photograph very difficult.[52]

This tree is the distinctive fastigiate type of black poplar, usually male, although I have seen female Lombardy poplars on a visit to Vienna in Austria, and it is probable that others exist elsewhere. A less columnar female version is found in Britain and Europe, which is thought to be a cross between a male Lombardy poplar and female black poplar,[53] and is known as *P. nigra* var

FIGURE 7.
Aerial view of the River Drome floodplain in France; it can also be seen that very little, if any, river engineering has taken place. The forests seen on the riverbanks are virtually unknown in Britain, although work is underway to recreate floodplain woodland.
JEAN-MICHEL FATON

Plantierensis.[54] The origins of the Lombardy poplar are uncertain. It is believed by some to have originated in Asia[55] and to have been introduced to Britain from the Lombardy area of Italy by Lord Rochford in 1758.[56] However, it may have been introduced prior to 1758 by the Duke of Argyll, as a particularly large specimen on his property was recorded by Loudon.[57] Others believe it to be a 'sport' of the normal form of black poplar[58] which has been extensively propagated and planted. A 'sport' can arise in two ways, either as an abnormal seedling or as a single abnormal branch on an otherwise normal tree.[59] The tree is highly susceptible to the foliage fungus *Marssonina populi-nigrae*, suggesting that it may be a distinct sub-species, as other black poplars do not appear to be affected by this disease.

The chronology of hybridisation

Of the hybrid black poplars, those cultivars known as Serotina, Eugenei, Gelrica, Heidemij, I–78, I–214, Marilandica, Regenerata and Robusta are found in Britain, either planted for ornamental purposes or as commercial plantation timber trees. The hybrid between *P. nigra* and *P. deltoides* was originally named *P. canadensis* in 1785 by Moench.[60] The name was misleading, in that it incorrectly suggested that the tree was of Canadian origin. Additionally, a common name for the tree, 'Black Italian Poplar', has resulted in confusion with *P. nigra* italica, the Lombardy poplar. For hybridisation with black poplar to occur naturally, it is essential for flowering times to coincide and those cultivars that readily hybridise with black poplar are shown in Table 1. Information given in the table results from unpublished observations by the Forestry Commission on specimens grown in a clone bank. It is believed that there are a number of trees which have undergone hybrid introgression, where a hybrid poplar has crossed with black poplar to produce a tree that is at least 25 per cent non-black poplar.[61]

Clone	*Sex*	*Hybridisation Risk*
P. x euramericana Heidemij	Male	Moderate
P. x euramericana Marilandica	Female	Moderate
P. x euramericana Regenerata	Female	High
P. x euramericana Robusta	Male	Moderate
P. nigra Italica	Male	Very high
P. nigra Plantierensis	Female	High
P. x berolinensis	Male and female	Moderate
P. x generosa x nigra	Male and female	High
P. x euramericana Geneva	Female	Moderate
P. x euramericana Rochester	Female	Moderate
P. trichocarpa	Female	Moderate
P. deltoides	Male and female	High
P. x euramericana Oxford	Male and female	Moderate
P. x euramericana Eugenei	Male and female	Moderate
P. x euramericana I–78 and I–214	Female	High

TABLE 1: Poplars capable of natural hybridisation (adapted from White, unpublished)

The historical nomenclature of black poplar

The earliest reference to the name 'black poplar' is found in Evelyn's classic seventeenth-century work *Sylva.*[62] However, poplar was previously recorded in medieval documents under the names popel, popelar or popular, as distinct from aspe (aspen) or abele (white poplar); this usage probably denotes black poplar,[63] as hybrid species were unknown until the mid eighteenth century.

The first occurrence of the east London place-name 'Poplar' was in 1327,[64] and the borough name, Poplar, may be derived from the large number of poplar trees growing in moist soil by the River Thames, many of which were still standing in 1720.[65] Again, it is probable that these were black poplars; at this time hybrid examples had yet to be introduced, and white poplars were known as 'abele'. Perhaps most importantly, the trees were situated on a floodplain, a location, as noted above, thought to be the species' natural habitat. A later article suggested that the singular name 'Poplar' indicates that only one distinctive specimen existed, which would have been 'held in view by those who passed along the great bend of the river between Limehouse and the Lea mouth'.[66]

A great variety of descriptive names have been applied to black poplar. Cook, writing in 1724, makes an explicit link between black poplar and damp habitats, noting that 'in most places [the tree] called the water poplar', is the 'same which some call the Black-poplar'.[67] Twentieth-century authorities list an assortment of regional names given to the tree. Grigson describes local names for black poplar thus: in Lancashire, due to dark knots in the wood, it was known as catfoot poplar; in Suffolk its name was the cotton-tree, because of the fluffy female seed; in Somerset it was known as the water poplar; and in Cambridgeshire, the willow poplar.[68] Gutch and Peacock mention that the black poplar, not the aspen, was known as the Shivver-tree in marshland areas such as parts of Lincolnshire,[69] whilst Edlin suggested that it was called 'black' to distinguish it from white and grey poplars; current feeling among many botanists is that its name derives from the dark appearance of its bark.[70]

Native or not?

The two sub-species of *P. nigra* that have been defined by phenotypic, rather than genotypic, characteristics, have well-defined geographical ranges. *P. nigra* subsp *betulifolia* is found in Britain and on the fringe of western Europe, whilst *P. nigra* subsp *nigra* is found throughout the remainder of Europe.[71]

P. nigra subsp *betulifolia* probably recolonised Britain during the post-glacial northerly tree migration, some 7,500 years BP. However, the absence of a fossil pollen record, as analysis cannot reliably differentiate between black and white poplar and aspen, coupled with the fact that *Populus* pollen is short-lived,[72] has resulted in some doubt as to its native status.[73] However, Huntley and Birks suggested that *P. nigra* was an early colonist of most sites in Europe during the Holocene, and do not specifically exclude Britain. Godwin mentions two Flandrian records of *P. nigra* L in charcoal of Neolithic and Saxon origin;[74] Turrill also states that *Populus* sp. charcoal was found in Neolithic deposits.[75] Pennington refers to *Populus* catkin scales in pollen studies, but as these were only found in the north-west of the British Isles, it is probable that they were aspen, rather than black poplar.[76] Clapham *et al.* suggested that the species may be native,[77] and later refined its origins to the river valleys in Britain, south of an imaginary line between the Mersey and Humber estuaries, with introductions in Cornwall and west Wales.[78] An argument in favour of its native status is the absence of *P. nigra* subsp *nigra* in Britain, suggesting a natural development independent of human intervention, as it is improbable that only one sub-species would have been introduced to Britain from Europe.

Whatever the true native status of the tree, it is evident that a great deal of human intervention has taken place with black poplar propagation, which may have occurred over some 1,000 years, and that the species has survived as a result of this intervention.

Current status of black poplar in Britain

Black poplar is thought to be one of Britain's most endangered trees.[79] Although around 7,000 are currently recorded (of which only about 600 are female), most of these trees are aged around 200 years, and therefore reaching the end of their natural lifespan. As a result, many trees are lost each year; in the county of Suffolk alone, almost one third of the population has been lost since 1987[80] and, since little planting or natural regeneration has occurred over the past two centuries, it is therefore possible that the species could become extinct within the next thirty years.

The plight of the tree was first highlighted by Edgar Milne-Redhead, a life-long black poplar enthusiast, who, upon his retirement from the Royal Botanic Gardens at Kew,[81] undertook a national survey of the tree between 1973 and 1988 (see Chapter Four).[82] By 1975, he had found some 1,000 trees,[83] although this number did not include the large populations in and around Manchester and the Vale of Aylesbury, as the mapping and recording of these (and other heavily populated areas) was more than one person could undertake.[84] The Biological Records Centre (BRC) at the Centre for Ecology and Hydrology (CEH) (formerly the Institute of Terrestrial Ecology (ITE)) has, in conjunction with Edgar Milne-Redhead, held records of the black poplar population in Britain and Ireland since 1973, the year Milne-Redhead commenced his survey.[85]

The recorded population remained fairly static until the species was brought more fully to the public's attention by a mention on Radio 4 by John White, which was followed with an article by Peter Roe published in 1994 in the *Daily Telegraph*.[86] Roe launched The Black Poplar Hunt and generated much public interest in the species (in conjunction with the Tree Council and the Forestry Commission), as a result of which the record expanded by some 250 trees. These were verified by John White, although it was found that many previously recorded trees had been lost.[87] Prior to Roe's article, Edgar Milne-Redhead had thought that only 1,000 trees remained; however, as a result of the interest generated in the 1990s, this gradually increased to around 2,500 (of which around 150 were known to be female).

Invertebrate association with black poplar

Druce lists the following invertebrates found in 1843 by Baxter on a black poplar in Oxfordshire: *Erysiphe adunca*, *Uredo populi*, *Erinaeum populinum* and *Sphaeria centocarpa*.[88] A study by Kennedy and Southwood found a total of 12 families of invertebrates (Acarina Eriophyidae (bud gall mite), Coleoptera, (beetles) Diptera Agromyzidae (true flies), Diptera Cecidomyidae (true flies), Heteroptera (land bugs), Homoptera Auchenorhyncha (true bugs), Homoptera Psylloidea (true bugs), Homoptera Aphidoidea (true bugs), Homoptera Coccoidea (true bugs), Hymenoptera Symphyta (sawflies) and 'macro' Lepidoptera (butterflies and moths)) on four species of poplar.[89]

FIGURE 8.
A sight which is sadly all too common; a tree which is over-mature and hollow throughout its centre is prone to wind-throw, as has happened to this specimen near Ludlow in Shropshire. Mourning its demise is Marianne Jones.
PETER NORMAN

FIGURE 9.
This is one of a lovely group of trees at Welford on Avon in Warwickshire. The photograph illustrates how fallen black poplars can embed themselves into the ground, take root and grow to form new trees.
FIONA COOPER

Unfortunately, no identification below family level was undertaken, and no distinction made between *Populus* species, but the study indicates the importance of the genus as invertebrate habitat.

During fieldwork in Hertfordshire, the following invertebrate fauna were observed on trees surveyed as part of my Ph.D. research: two species of froghopper (family Cercopidae) and an uncommon bark beetle, *Dorytomus longimanus,* which was identified by Trevor James. In addition, the scarce bark beetle species *D. filirostris, D. ictor* (bark beetles), *Rhynchaenus populi* (leaf miner), *Byctiscus populi* (bark beetle) and *Saperda carcharias* (longhorn beetle) have been associated with black poplar,[90] although these species were not observed during fieldwork.

Decline of black poplar in Britain

The black poplar population in Britain is thought to have declined for a variety of reasons. These include the clearance of floodplain forest, land drainage and river engineering operations, an unequal number of male and female trees, unsuitable ground conditions for seed set, the unpopularity of female trees among those planting or managing the species and the breeding and introduction of a faster-growing, more commercially viable hybrid species *P. x canadensis.*

If, as most writers appear to suggest, black poplar is a native species, and was a component of floodplain forest, the clearance of such woodland in the Neolithic period and thereafter for agricultural purposes would have dramatically reduced numbers of the tree.[91] Much later, as land drainage became widespread in the seventeenth and eighteenth centuries,[92] the wet river margins and the bare wet soil conditions necessary for black poplar seed to set were removed. This practice continued until the late 1980s, when concern arose about over-production in agriculture and the destruction of wetland areas.[93] River engineering, involving the straightening and deepening of river channels in order to carry excess water away as quickly as possible, was carried out in many locations to alleviate flooding.[94] These activities also involved the removal of in-stream and riparian vegetation, as well as riverside trees,[95] and it is likely that many black poplars fell victim to this type of clearance.

The paucity of female specimens, coupled with unsuitable ground conditions for seed set, even where males and females grow together, has resulted in an almost total lack of natural regeneration. A study of the seed viability of P. deltoides by Braatne *et al.* found that seed was only viable for one to two weeks,[96] whilst Turrill states that black poplar seed must germinate 'very soon after maturity'.[97] However, Van Splunder *et al.* found that 10 per cent of *P. nigra* seed germinated after 30 days' storage.[98] In an *ex situ* study, it was found that no mortality occurred in a greenhouse experiment with seedlings,[99] suggesting that environmental conditions are contributory factors in establishing seed set. An additional problem is that the fluff surrounding the seed prevents it from embedding into the ground.

The fluffy seed produced by females may have also influenced the male to female ratio in Britain, as female trees were unpopular among farmers since the fluff was considered to 'adversely affect the appearance of market produce', particularly lettuce.[100] It also causes a nuisance to soft-fruit growers and to farmers at haymaking time.[101] A recent survey in Italy found a similar male to female ratio to that in Britain,[102] suggesting that the fluff may also have been unpopular in parts of Europe, possibly for similar reasons. However, of 70 randomly sampled trees from six natural stands in France, 33 were male and 37 were female,[103] suggesting that the male to female ratio is more balanced in France. In assessing such ratios, it must not be forgotten that the species is not as widely planted in Europe as it is in Britain, with many natural populations still existing. Some writers feel that fluffy seed would not have been a problem for medieval farmers and that the problem has been exaggerated as a way of explaining the paucity of females.[104] However, the planting of males does appear to have been favoured in certain areas, and two individual female trees are known to have been destroyed because of the inconvenience fluff caused to motorists: the first in a lay-by in Gloucestershire[105] and the second in a pub car park in Worcestershire.[106] In addition, the planting of males may have been favoured for practical reasons; in *Populus* sp. short-rotation energy plantations, males are known to yield higher dry weight mass than females,[107] although a recent study has indicated that females grow better than males in wetter sites.[108]

A potential major factor in the decline of black poplar was the introduction, thought by Loudon to have been in 1769,[109] of a faster-growing, more commercially viable hybrid, then known as *P. serotina*[110] (a name now used to describe a male cultivar), or *P. x canadensis* Moench. This name was abandoned in 1950 by the International Poplar Commission and replaced by *P. x euramericana* (Dode) Guinier, as it was felt that the former name implied a specific geographical origin.[111] The species is a cross between American *P. deltoides* Marshall and European *P. nigra* L (the subspecies of the latter parent is unknown). The commercial use of this hybrid led to a decline in the planting of the native species, which was thereafter largely forgotten, other than for occasional hedgerow and urban planting.[112] Thus, as noted above, an absence of regeneration requirements for seed set and a lack of planting have resulted in an even-aged population, with many trees nearing the end of their natural lifespan; the natural result is many fallen old trees (Figure 8). However, despite the decline, it is possible that the tree was never common in Britain, even in the seventeenth century. Evelyn observed that the 'black poplar grows rarely with us', whereas 'divers stately ones of these I remember about the banks of Po in Italy'.[113]

The reputed ease of hybridisation with certain non-native poplar species, whose flowering time coincides with black poplar, combined with the efficiency of wind pollination, has meant that a number of trees have suffered genetic pollution. These are morphologically similar to *P. nigra* subsp *betulifolia* but are in fact backcrosses,[114] and many have been incorrectly recorded as the native sub-species. The difficulties encountered when identifying black poplar are exemplified by the specimen incorrectly described in *A Flora of Cumbria* as England's most northerly black poplar, on the banks of the River Eden at Langwathby[115] (the most northerly recorded example is in Berwickshire). Although the leaves on this particular tree have all the characteristics of being a true black poplar, the same cannot be said of the general jizz of the tree, as it has a hybrid habit: its twigs are not upturning and its bark does not have the characteristic deep, uneven fissuring. These finds were very disappointing, as the tree is in the classic location and is most picturesque; I can only conclude that this is an example of a genetically polluted individual.

Rather disturbingly, in recent years, the black poplar may have become a victim of its own popularity; the scarcity of the species and, in particular, female individuals, make them very popular with enthusiasts, and I am aware of more than one landowner who has become a little weary of streams of visitors to their trees. Whilst this has probably not led to the loss of a great number of trees, one landowner in Berkshire has in fact felled a tree to prevent large numbers of people from visiting his land.[116]

Despite these problems, the tree has its own strategies for survival and is able to propagate by vegetative means (Figure 9). Many trees that have fallen will, if left, produce roots from trunks and survive for many more years; downsweeping branches often embed themselves into the ground. It is thought that some trees, having fallen and regenerated in this manner, may be several hundred years of age.[117] It is possible that riverside trees may have regenerated in a similar manner, as branches and shoots which break off and wash downstream are embedded in riverbanks. Again, it is possible that such trees are relicts of wild colonies, some hundreds of years old. A genetic study of riverside willows in Germany found that trees along the stretch of river studied were genetically identical, and the authors concluded that they originated from the lost branches of a single individual which had become embedded downstream.[118]

CHAPTER TWO

The Black Poplar in History

Black poplar in historical texts

During the Middle Ages, the term 'black poplar' does not appear to have been used. In this period, however, general references to 'poplar' abound, and Rackham takes them to mean black poplar.[1] In 1310, a John Petye cut down one poplar in Nowton, Suffolk, without permission and was fined two shillings; in 1422 an ancient, decayed poplar tree was condemned for growing too far over the king's highway at Great Canfield in Essex. The timber was valuable in medieval times: for example, in 1399 12 shillings was paid for the branches of a poplar felled at Writtle in Essex.[2] Linnard reports that tenants in Wales were required to plant 180 trees during their tenure, and the stipulated trees were 'either oak, ash, elm, poplar or walnut'.[3] No mention is made in these cases of the exact species involved, but the trees in question may have been black poplar since hybrid poplars had not been introduced to Britain at that time and it is unlikely that a white poplar (thought to have been introduced from Holland during the twelfth century) would have been mature enough either to be decayed or viable for timber in the 1300s. In addition, the white poplar appears to have been known by the name abel or abele during the Middle Ages. The earliest detailed historical record that refers specifically to black poplar, as opposed to the more general term 'poplar', is John Evelyn's classic work of 1664, *Sylva*, in which he discussed propagation, distribution and timber use.[4]

By the eighteenth and nineteenth centuries, different species of poplar were commonly distinguished from one another. Linnard notes that Hindes' forest nursery at Felindre near Newcastle Emlyn list 3,000 black poplars in their 1815 inventory, and describes the planting between 1804 and 1810 of 75,000 poplars in Denbighshire, but states that these were hybrid species. He also discusses a small plantation of black poplar in Tre-ffin in 1774, grown to analyse stem growth, where it was found that unpruned trees with the greatest growing space produced most stem volume.[5] Threlkeld, writing in 1727, briefly mentions that 'there is a sort of poplar called black', but does not elaborate upon numbers or distribution.[6]

Despite the growing transparency in the terms used to distinguish poplars, it can be seen from more recent literature that considerable confusion surrounds the correct identification of the black poplar. Edlin appears to be uncertain about the native status of the tree, stating in 1945 that it 'is indigenous throughout Europe, and occurs in a wild state in Britain',[7] but unfortunately illustrates a hybrid poplar. However, by 1956, he argued that three or four poplars are probably native to Britain, of which black poplar is one.[8] In 1985, he reiterated his belief that the tree is one of Britain's 'few native kinds', and regarded it as an uncommon species.[9] Step, in 1940, considered the tree a 'common introduced species' and, again, the accompanying illustration is in fact a hybrid species,[10] suggesting that he may have been unaware of the identity of the true black poplar. Edwards, writing in 1962, lists *P. nigra* subsp *betulifolia* as the Manchester poplar, and says it is widely planted, but he does not confer native or non-native status upon it.[11] Further confusion arose with the publication of *Atlas of the British Flora* in 1962,[12] which included many records of hybrid poplars, giving a completely misleading distribution throughout Britain.[13] The well-known dendrologist, Alan Mitchell, regarded the tree as native to central and south-east England, and acknowledged its scarcity.[14]

Historical timber uses

Prior to the species' decline in Britain, and the introduction of the more commercially viable hybrid species, black poplar was an important timber tree with a diverse range of uses. However, the distribution of pollards and standards throughout the country is unequal, suggesting that its use as a timber tree was not universal. For example, whilst many individuals in Herefordshire and Worcestershire are pollarded, Shropshire has pollarded trees at only one site, where five pollards and two coppiced trees exist (excluding those trees that have been trimmed for safety reasons). Pollards are abundant in hedgerows in Derbyshire, Herefordshire, East Anglia, the Vale of Aylesbury (discussed in greater detail in Chapter Three), Gloucestershire and Somerset, despite Rackham's statement that 'pollards are now uncommon except in Eastern England'.[15] Approximately 90 pollarded individuals are to be found on Castlemorton Common, Worcestershire, and are regarded by some as 'probably the best collection left'. However, all these trees are male and are probably planted examples, as they are located in small groups near houses. The trees were pollarded at differing times in order to provide poles of varying sizes. Commoners used young branches for rough basketry, older poles for fencing, wattle and daub walls, and ladders, together with fuel wood. The Malvern Hills Conservators have undertaken a propagation programme of these trees to ensure their continued survival.[16] Rackham notes that poplar pollards were put to various uses: poles from trees in Brandon, Suffolk, were used for flooring the rabbit warren lodge in 1386–7; a wayside poplar in Writtle, Essex, was shredded (their sides and tops trimmed, leaving only the trunk), possibly for animal fodder;[17] the Bishop of Ely utilised timber from black and white poplar growing at Brandon, but it is not clear how it was used.[18] Timber from poplar was clearly highly prized: in 1399, 12d was paid for the branches of a tree felled at Writtle in Essex.[19]

Timber from black poplar has fire resistant and shock absorbent properties. The former makes it less than ideal for fuel:[20] Selby regarded the timber as almost useless for this purpose and thought, rather, that early summer shoots were dried and stored for winter animal fodder.[21] In a similar vein, the owner of two female trees and one male tree in Herefordshire thought the wood was utilised in hop kilns because of its resistance to fumes.[22] The slow-burning characteristics of the timber were reputedly put to use by a Shropshire householder, who rather uncharitably gave it to his servants for firewood in their quarters,[23] whilst another Shropshire householder used it as flooring in the servant's quarters to prevent accidental fires.[24] However, alternative views exist: Trimmer suggested that many trees in Norfolk were shredded for fuel wood; he may have been following Evelyn, who considered that loppings taken in January were used for firewood.[25]

However, the timber is highly suitable for a vast array of items, such as bowls and other wooden vessels, small rafters, railings, baskets, cart floors, fence poles, plant supports, spar-gadds (used in thatching), aircraft ribs, clogs, clothes pegs, railway brake blocks, cruck frames and flooring in agricultural buildings; its bark was used for tanning and fishing net floats.[26] The Roman scientist and scholar Pliny recommended the use of black poplar as support for vines,[27] and Evelyn also mentions this practice, which continued in Italy until the last century.[28] The wood was also used for making fruit and vegetable 'chip' baskets; indeed, poplar (probably hybrid) timber is still used for the construction of lightweight wooden vegetable boxes in Europe, albeit less frequently, now that plastic is commonly used.[29] Its use has been noted in particularly interesting contexts: a submerged, hollow trunk used as a well lining was found in Viking York excavations,[30] and arrows found on the ship *Mary Rose* were discovered to be made from black poplar, and were alleged to be from a tree still growing in the town of Portsmouth, although it is highly unlikely that this connection can ever be proven. A wooden chest dating to the fourteenth century in the church at East Bergholt in Suffolk has a lid clearly made from the hollow trunk of a mature black poplar, probably aged around 200 years, which would predate any introduction of white or hybrid poplar (Figure 10).[31] Cook highlighted the commercial importance of the tree, suggesting that 'if you set one of these worth a half penny, if they grow they will bring you that yearly for twenty years or more'.[32] In Herefordshire folklore, poplar appears to be favoured over other timber species, as evidenced in this anonymous rhyme:

> Cut me green and keep me dry
> And I will oak or elm defy[33]

The shock-absorbent qualities of black poplar wood, noted above, made a peculiarly suitable for the construction of carts.[34] The owner of 18 black poplars near Crickhowell in Brecon believes that the trees planted in his

FIGURE 10.
Fourteenth-century chest at East Bergholt church in Suffolk. The lid of the chest is constructed from a hollowed-out black poplar half-log.
FIONA COOPER

FIGURE 11.
Pen and ink illustration of the black poplar and oak-framed barn from Cholstrey in Herefordshire, which was reconstructed at Avoncroft Museum, Bromsgrove in the early 1970s.
MICHAEL TENNYSON

FIGURE 12.
Gable end of Cholstrey barn (*c.* 1580), showing the cruck frame, which was probably constructed from black poplar; the rather jagged appearance of the timbers is due to bossing and burring, found on many mature trees.
FIONA COOPER

FIGURE 13.
A beautiful ornamental bowl turned from a black poplar burr.
JOHN WHITE

woodland were utilised for the cart industry that operated in the River Usk valley some 200 years ago.[35] John Constable depicted the tree in his famous painting *The Hay Wain* in 1821, albeit in a stylised manner, and it is possible that the cart in the painting was constructed with black poplar timber.[36] And with the advent of the railways and aeroplanes, the uses of black poplar were further extended: Milne-Redhead suggests that the timber was used not only for the floors of farm wagons, but also those of railway trucks, and for the spars and ribs of aircraft.[37]

As already stated, black poplar timber is a fire-resistant timber, due to the low levels of volatile organic compounds (VOCs) present, and was known to have been used in the construction of agricultural buildings, both as a frame and as flooring. Within the counties of Herefordshire and Worcestershire, five barns have been found with cruck frames constructed from poplar wood, although the species has not been confirmed.[38] Cruck-framed buildings were one of the earliest forms of building, with some dating back to the thirteenth century, and were constructed from naturally curved tree trunks, which were split and placed in reverse to form an arch. A cross beam was usually pegged into each side of this arch to achieve greater stability. Mature black poplar was particularly suitable for this purpose, due to its tendency to produce curved trunks. A barn from Cholstrey, near Leominster in Herefordshire (Figure 11), which was reconstructed in 1972 at the Avoncroft Museum in Bromsgrove, is a cruck-framed building constructed from poplar timber, (identified at the Royal Botanical Gardens, Kew). Although the species is not confirmed, it is probably black poplar, since the cruck-frame was constructed from a mature tree, evidenced by the indentations left by burrs and bosses (Figure 12) which are clearly visible on close inspection of the frame. The precise date of construction of the barn is unknown, but carpentry details such as the angle and dimensions of the braces in the wall frame suggest a date sometime in the sixteenth century; since hybrid poplars were not introduced until the middle of the eighteenth century, this date-range would appear to confirm the use of black poplar. The remainder of the frame was built of oak.[39] The barn is one of five similarly constructed cruck barns in north-west Herefordshire.[40]

In view of the current, rather alarming, rate of loss of mature trees, it would be gratifying to find ways of utilising the timber. One of the most appealing uses is that of turned artefacts made from the burrs found on many ancient trees. Although extremely light in weight, they make magnificent ornamental bowls and vases (Figure 13). It should be stressed, however, that timber should only be taken from fallen trees, and those still standing should be preserved for as long as possible.

Medicinal applications of black poplar

Historically, black poplar, along with many other plants, has been used to treat a variety of injuries and conditions. Balsam from the buds of black poplar was thought to be beneficial in treating bruises, inflammation and gout:[41] in the fifteenth century an ointment made from black poplar buds, known as *Unguentum Populeon*, was used by the herbalist, Gerard, for these purposes.[42] Nicholas Culpeper, the seventeenth-century herbalist, believed that 'The water that drops from the hollows of this tree takes away warts, wheals and breakings out of the body', and thought that the tree provided a treatment for 'falling sickness'.[43] The view that black poplar could be used to treat warts remained current in the late nineteenth century, when Friend mentions the washing of warts with water collected from black poplar.[44] By the early twentieth century the use of black poplar was still prevalent in local folklore; in Lincolnshire the practice of tying a lock of hair to a black poplar branch as a cure for ague, a shaking fever, was common.[45] Modern herbalists believe that the species can be used for the treatment of arthritis, bronchitis, haemorrhoids and rheumatic diseases,[46] and there is perhaps a need for further research to be conducted into its medicinal applications.

Black poplar in literature

There are two principal references to black poplar in English literature during the nineteenth century. The poem *Binsey Poplars*, by Gerard Manley Hopkins, was written about the felling of poplars at Binsey, near Oxford, in 1879. Hopkins was sensitive to 'beauty in natural objects' and, in referring to 'my aspens dear', clearly feels a sense of personal loss.[47] Although he uses the name aspen, rather than poplar, this is probably for alliterative purposes, and this poem captures, as well as words are able, the delightful sound and appearance of a quivering black poplar on a breezy day.

My aspens dear, whose airy cages quelled,
Quelled or quenched in leaves the leaping sun,
All felled, felled, all are felled;
Of a fresh and following folded rank
Not spared, not one
That dandled a sandalled
Shadow that swam or sank
On meadow and river and wind-wandering weed-winding bank.

It appears that not all the poplars at this site were felled, as John Jobling of the Forestry Commission recorded a tree at this site in 1952, which is listed on the national record.

The poem *The Poplar Field*, by William Cowper, written in 1784, also refers to felled poplars:[48]

The Poplars are fell'd, farewell to the shade
And the whispering sound of the cool colonnade,
The winds play no longer, and sing in the leaves,
Nor Ouse in his bosom their image receives.

Twelve years have elaps'd since I last took a view
Of my favourite field and the bank where they grew,
And now in the grass behold they are laid,
And the tree is my seat that once lent me shade.

The blackbird has fled to another retreat
Where the hazels afford him a screen from the heat,
And the scene where his melody charm'd me before,
Resounds with his sweet floating ditty no more.

My fugitive years are all hasting away
And I must ere long lie as lowly as they,
With a turf on my breast, and a stone at my head,
Ere another such grove shall arise in its stead.

'Tis a sight to engage me, if anything can,
To muse on the perishing pleasures of man,
Though his life be a dream, his enjoyments, I see,
Have a being less durable ever than he.

Whilst both pieces of work clearly refer to the felling of trees, there appear to be differences in the motives for writing. Manley Hopkins' work lays more emphasis upon the ecological devastation caused by the loss of trees, whereas Cowper's writing, although also concerned with ecological damage, displays a concern about his own mortality as he regrets that he will not last to see 'another such grove ... rise in its stead'.

Black poplar in folklore

Black poplar has held an important place in folklore for many centuries, and appears to have had particular significance in the Ancient World. Indeed, Greek myth describes the beginning of the species: Phaeton and his sisters pestered their father, Helios, the sun god, to allow Phaeton to drive the chariot of the sun for a day. Very reluctantly, Helios agreed. Unfortunately, Phaeton could not control the horses and drove too close to the sun. Zeus, the greatest of the Greek gods, was furious at such stupidity and threw Phaeton into the River Eridanus. His grieving sisters stood on the bank until the gods took pity on them and turned them into the first black poplars. The legend is said to explain the bud exudate observed on the species, where the tree, according to Paterson, 'almost weeps with sticky balsam'.[49] Graves also discusses the Phaeton legend, but suggests that the trees were alders, rather than poplars.[50]

According to the Roman poet Virgil (10–19 BC), in *The Aeneid*, the poplar was sacred to Hercules, and he is said to have worn it on his way to the underworld. Virgil described how the underside of the leaves absorbed the 'sweat of his brow', whilst the upper side remained dark, like the underworld. Although the precise species is unclear, it is probable that Virgil was referring to black poplar; his description of the undersides of the leaves as silvery and the upper sides as dark green is an accurate description of black poplar leaf characteristics.[51] Graves suggests how Aegira, the home of Mother Earth, in Achaea in Ancient Greece, may have been named after the black poplar (the tree belongs to the Aigeiros group of poplars), 'a tree sacred to heroes', and suggests that the tree was sacred to Mother Earth in pre-Hellenic Greece as a funereal tree; in his play *Casina*, the Roman playwright Titus Maccius Plautus refers to black poplar as 'standing for loss of hope',[52] which may link with its funereal associations. Indeed, Mabey goes so far as to suggest this connection as a reason for the name 'black poplar'.[53]

More recently, black poplar, in common with other plants, has been associated with the elements and was reputed to have supernatural or magical powers: Friend, writing in the late nineteenth century, discusses the association of some plants with the power to produce rain, and includes black poplar amongst them;[54] the tree has also been associated with the wind,[55] probably as a result of the noise made by its rustling leaves. In Germany, young girls used to place a lock of hair under the bark of a black poplar, in the hope that the rapid growth characteristics of the tree would transfer to the growth of their hair.[56] The magical powers attributed to the tree include the ability to 'shield and resist', to help with speech and language, and to bring monetary good fortune. Friend discusses its use as a 'soporiferous medicine' and suggests witches may have used it as an ointment to enable them to fly.[57] On a more sinister note, the crimson male catkins have been christened Devil's Fingers, and in some parts of Britain it is considered unlucky to pick them up.[58]

The Arbor Tree

The most famous black poplar in Britain, the Arbor Tree at Aston-on-Clun in Shropshire (Figure 14), is decorated with flags every 29 May (Oak Apple Day), to commemorate the wedding of two villagers, John Marston and Mary Carter, in 1786,[59] and is the only remaining tree-dressing ceremony in Britain. Prior to its demise in September 1995, the tree was one of Britain's oldest black poplars, as it is known to date back to 1715.[60] An elaborate ceremony took place on 16 December 1995 following the destruction of the original tree by windthrow (Figure 15), in which Roy Lancaster and the Bishop of Ludlow planted a replacement scion from the old tree at the tree's original site (Figure 16).[61]

The tree stands on what was once the village green,[62] alongside a stream, in an area which would have been the stream's floodplain prior to the creation of the village. It was previously known as The Bride's Tree,[63] probably referring to the wedding of John Marston and Mary Carter, although there is a possibility that the name relates to St. Bridget, or 'Brid', the Celtic fertility goddess; however, this latter suggestion is pure speculation. The earliest written reference to the Arbor Tree was made by Hopesay Parish Council in 1898, where it was spelt 'Arbour'.[64] The name was changed to 'Arbor' in 1954,[65] perhaps at the behest of Tom Beardsley (see below), who preferred the latter spelling.[66] The earliest written reference to the custom of dressing the tree was

FIGURE 14.
One of the oldest photographs in existence of the famous Arbor Tree at Aston-on-Clun in Shropshire. Taken in 1911, it clearly shows that the tree had recently undergone surgery.
COURTESY OF ROSIE EVANS

made comparatively recently, by J. E. Auden in 1912, who discussed the decoration which took place to commemorate the wedding, although he does not make mention of the tree's name.[67] The contemporary celebrations include a wedding pageant involving local children as the bride and bridegroom, who are escorted to the tree by a procession of villagers (Figure 17).

Several versions of the reasons behind the ceremony have evolved over the past 300 years. The most straightforward is that the tree was decorated simply to commemorate the wedding. More complex versions of the tale suggest that Mary Carter saw the bedecked tree and was so delighted with it that she contributed to the annual festivities; a sovereign was given to each of the village dwellers as part of the celebration and travellers could refresh themselves with food at the inn. Indeed, Hole doubts that the dressing of the Arbor Tree began as 'a Georgian wedding compliment', and suggests that Mary Carter made her endowment to maintain what was already a long-established custom.[68] Bailey and others have suggested that the flag dressing ceremony may have originated as a superstitious protection against witches;[69] the roots of such a belief may lie in an old Herefordshire custom of decorating birch saplings with red and white streamers and placing them outside stables to prevent witches riding the horses.[70]

The pagan practice of tree dressing was revived by Charles II in 1660, on Oak Apple Day, to commemorate his restoration,[71] and the day was declared a public holiday.[72] There are possibilities that Arbor Day was attached to Oak Apple Day or that the wedding coincided with fertility rites conducted in late May, and Mabey suggests that it is likely that the royal association has succeeded an earlier pagan tradition of tree worship.[73] Some writers have entertained the rather unlikely possibility that John Marston used fertility powers associated with the Arbor Tree on his second wife, as his first marriage had been childless (the second marriage to Mary subsequently produced four

FIGURE 15.
A local child surveys the devastation, in September 1995, of the fallen Arbor Tree. The trunk of the tree is now in possession of Paul Hand, whose geese have been known to nest in it; perhaps its powers of fertility live on.
DAVE PHILLIPS

children),[74] although it is possible that the wedding was arranged to coincide with spring fertility rites. In the 1950s it became a tradition to present a cutting to the child bride and groom who re-enact the wedding ceremony on Arbor Day in May.[75] Brides who so desired were also given cuttings, although this custom no longer continues, largely due to the fact that it had become something of an embarrassment locally; it was felt that the ceremony had become rather too pagan and thus unacceptable to the Church. Indeed, the minutes of the Parish Council record that a letter had been received from Norfolk, in Virginia, USA, which contained one dollar for a cutting.[76] Such incidents resulted in a downscaling of the ceremony in the early 1960s, in order to reduce the emphasis that had been placed upon fertility links.

Despite the apparent success of the tree as a fertility symbol for John and Mary Marsden, ill fortune plagued the family in later years, culminating in the

last of the line committing suicide in the 1950s, following which the Oaker estate was broken up and sold on a piecemeal basis. Hopesay Parish Council then took over responsibility for the tree.[77] The tree now has its own committee who organise Arbor Day and are ensuring the continuance of the custom.

However, it should be made clear that no documentary evidence has yet been found to confirm any link with fertility rites, or the dressing of the tree prior to the wedding in 1786, and such statements are purely conjecture. It is noteworthy that the Arbor Tree was first associated with fertility in the mid 1950s, coinciding with the arrival of Tom Beardsley (also known as Tom Clun) in the village as the village policeman. He may have been influenced by Derbyshire traditions such as well dressing and Garland King Day; but,

FIGURE 16.
The new Arbor Tree, a scion of the original, was planted in December 1995, and surrounded with a fence, seating and information board, rather to the chagrin of some enthusiasts who would have preferred the remaining stump to have been given the chance to regenerate.
COURTESY OF ROSIE EVANS

FIGURE 17.
Local children engaged in the wedding pageant re-enactment on Arbor Day in Aston-on-Clun.
MARIANNE JONES

regardless of his motivation, he became very interested in the tree and its traditions and wrote *The Ballad of the Arbor Tree.*[78] It is evident from the content of the verse that the Arbor Tree was very important to Tom Beardsley and the villagers of Aston on Clun, and remains so to this day.

In Aston Clun I stand, a tree,
A Poplar dressed, like a ship at sea,
Lonely link with an age long past:
Of Arbor Trees, I am the last

Since seventeen-eighty-six, My Day
Is write, the twenty ninth of May.
When new flags fly and we rejoice,
New life has stilled harsh Winter's voice.

To greet a Squire's lovely bride
Did tenants dress my boughs with pride?
But Old Wives say, my flags are worn
To mark the day an heir was born.

Wise men, mellow o'er evening ale,
Old feuds and wicked deeds retail.
Thanksgiving dressed my arms, they say
For Peace, when blood feuds died away.

Did here! My father mark the rite
Of Shepherds, gone with world's first light?
Was England merrie neath his shade
Till crop-Hair'd Cromwell joy forbade?

In sixteen-sixty with the Spring
Came Merry Charles the exiled king.
Did he proclaim May twenty-nine
'Arbor Day' for revelry and wine?

And Shepherds, plagued with pox and chills
Turn to the old ways of the hills,
To 'Mystic Poplar', to renew
Fertility in field and ewe?

Stand I, for Ancient ways, for Birth,
For Love, for Peace, for Joy and Mirth
Riddle my riddle as you will
I stand for good and not for ill.

And if my dress your fancy please
Help my flags to ride the breeze
That you with me, will in the Sun,
Welcome all, to the Vale of Clun.

The third line of the penultimate verse suggests that he intended readers of the ballad to place their own interpretations upon the meaning of the Arbor Tree, perhaps indicating that he was uncertain of the origins of Arbor Day. Indeed, the various interpretations of Arbor Tree traditions discussed above may be cultural constructions placed by local people upon the tree and its associated celebrations. Tsouvalis-Gerber discusses how subjective meanings can be ascribed to nature, and how this results from a longing for time gone by and a wish to preserve traces left behind by our species.[79] As Watkins says of the Sherwood Oaks, they have been 'prodded and probed', 'lopped and pollarded', 'exploited and felled'; they have undergone 'archaeological experiment and aesthetic reflection'; and have been used for fuel and timber. Throughout all these changing layers of value and meaning, which are gained and lost over time, onlookers remain 'innocent of their ancestry and antiquity'.[80] It can be argued that changing meanings are as acceptable for the Arbor Tree as for the Sherwood Oaks, as the former has undoubtedly undergone similar shifts in perception and meaning.

The commemorative tea towel sold at the Arbor Day celebration carries the following anonymous verse, acknowledging the tree's supposed fertility associations:

> Since long ago the "brides" Arbor Tree
> Has claimed to enhance fertility
>
> An age old tradition that holds the key
> Is to sit beneath and touch the tree.

My own view is that the tree dressing ceremony predated the wedding, perhaps dating back to the local celebrations of Royal Oak Day (Oak Apple Day) from 1660, or as a derivation of the ancient custom of tying rags to trees in order to ensure the granting of wishes, and that the association with fertility rites perhaps arose as a result of Tom Beardsley's beliefs.

The Hanging Tree

Trees were used as the earliest form of gallows; prisoners were either hauled up manually by the hangman or raised by a ladder or a cart. There are still some hanging trees in existence in Britain, as, for example, at Weeping Cross near Stafford.[81] It was usual to select a robust tree for this purpose; in Scotland, sycamore was the favoured species for use as a hanging tree, as its branches were unlikely to snap.[82] Perhaps surprisingly, in view of the species' notoriously brittle branches, a black poplar, next to the area still known as Gallows Bank, in Ludlow, Shropshire, was used as a hanging tree. The field used to be known at the Waretree Field, so-named after the 'wartree' or gallows; the tree stood on the skyline, and was visible from many parts of the town,[83] allowing the condemned person an uninterrupted view of the church from the gallows. Weyman refers to various hangings there from 1556 to 1606, together with

NEWENT
THE SCARR

FIGURE 18.
Dick Whittington's Tree at Botloe's Green, near Newent in Gloucestershire; enormous amounts of campaigning by the villagers to obtain a Tree Preservation Order and village green status for the tree sadly failed, due to the intransigent attitude of the local council.
FIONA COOPER

FIGURE 19.
The valuable tree at Powick, near Worcester. Prior to the development of the south Worcester bypass the tree stood, rather neglected, in a hedgerow along a quiet lane.
MARIANNE JONES

account entries dating back to 1576 relating to payments for setting up the Gallows Tree and carrying the ladder to the tree;[84] Lloyd describes how Francis Vaughan was sentenced to hang for the crime of 'picking purses'.[85] As black poplar is a comparatively short-lived species (generally no more than 250–300 years), it is likely that another tree preceded the one which stood there until recently. This raises the question of what species the original tree was; the black poplar is unlikely to have been planted as a direct replacement for the gallows tree as it would not have been mature and strong enough to use for that purpose for some time. It is therefore possible that the original gallows tree was in fact a specimen of another species. In more recent times, prior to its demise, the black poplar was used to support a rope swing for the local children. Although the tree has fallen, a number of cuttings have been grown to ensure the continuity of this culturally important tree,[86] and a rock on the site of the fallen tree could be regarded as commemorating the site.

Dick Whittington's Tree

A magnificent solitary male black poplar, full of character, and known locally as Dick Whittington's Tree, stands on the remains of the village green at Botloe's Green, near Newent in Gloucestershire (Figure 18). This tree has been the subject of much publicity, following threats to the green and the tree by a local businessman seeking permission to run a skip hire operation from a property adjacent to the green.[87] The name 'Dick Whittington's Tree' was bestowed upon the tree for publicity purposes by a group of local residents who campaigned for village green status and a tree preservation order for the poplar, in order to afford protection from possible damage as a result of the commercial operation. Unfortunately, despite seven years' campaigning, they were unsuccessful and finally acknowledged defeat in 2002.

This tree appears to have particular significance within its immediate environs. The green on which it stands is situated on a prominent piece of ground, at a meeting point of tracks and roads, several of which are shown on the Newent tithe map of 1838, on which map the tree is also marked. In addition, early editions of Ordnance Survey maps show a small settlement, which may have developed here in late or post medieval times. 'Botloe' is derived from the Anglo-Saxon words *Bota*, a personal name, and *hlaw*, meaning a mound, tumulus or hill, and gives its name to the Botloe Hundred[88] (an administrative county sub-division dating back to the tenth century). Hundred meeting places were generally in prominent places and were often marked with a stone, tree or tumulus, which would perhaps explain the presence of the ancient black poplar on the green. The tree was marked on a map dated 1810, when it was probably a mature tree of local importance;[89] it may have replaced an older, fallen specimen. The 1838 tithe map names the adjacent field as the Hundred Field, adding further weight to the argument that the green was the meeting place for the Botloe Hundred.[90]

Although the name 'Dick Whittington's Tree' was only given in recent times, it does have a degree of historical accuracy. Dick Whittington's father, William de Whitington, was an important local landowner in nearby Pauntley in the fourteenth century,[91] and it is likely that he would have attended meetings of the Botloe Hundred on the green, possibly with young Dick accompanying him.

A very valuable tree

Lastly, I would like to mention what is probably Britain's most expensive black poplar. Prior to the development of the south Worcester bypass, the tree, a neglected pollard, stood in a hedgerow alongside a quiet lane from Worcester to Powick (Figure 19). The remaining trunk was hollow, in which it was possible to stand, and the tree had survived attacks from vandals, including one attempt to set fire to it (Figure 20). However, the advent of the bypass put its future severely in jeopardy, as it stood in the path of the road. Thankfully, Worcestershire Wildlife Trust stepped in, and the planners agreed to construct a traffic island to contain the tree, at a cost of approximately £20,000.[92] The tree was pollarded to safeguard its health, and now thrives on the island (Figure 21). In fact, root damage suffered by the tree has resulted in a sucker producing a young tree nearby, which will, I hope, be allowed to grow to maturity.

FIGURE 20.
Hollow interior of the Powick traffic island tree, which has survived vandalism and arson, and will hopefully live for many more years.
PETER NORMAN

FIGURE 21.
The newly pollarded Powick traffic island tree, showing vigorous growth; the tree is adapting well to its new environment, which may have afforded extra protection since it is now less accessible.
PETER NORMAN

CHAPTER THREE

The Black Poplar in the Landscape

Today, black poplars are generally found outside their natural habitat of lowland floodplain. A large proportion of trees extant in rural Britain are planted in hedgerows, often some distance from rivers and even, in some cases, at altitude. This is true of both isolated trees and of trees in large groups, such as those in the Vale of Aylesbury and south Derbyshire. However, they are still dramatic landscape features, regardless of their location and numbers. Black poplar has been utilised both as an urban and a rural tree, although perhaps to a lesser degree in the latter situation, where it is generally found as an isolated specimen, or in small groups of two or three. In rural areas they are rarely found in groups of more than ten, although there are exceptions to this generalisation.

In certain areas of the Britain – namely Buckinghamshire and the North West, around Manchester and Lancashire – black poplar is a common sight. In fact, in the Vale of Aylesbury it is the most common tree in the area, with at least 4,500 – 5,000 individuals, many of which are planted in hedgerows. In almost all other areas of Britain, however, it is considerably more rare than, for example, yews, of which almost every parish in Britain has at least one, either in a churchyard, by a cottage, or as part of formal planting in gardens.[1]

There are many black poplars around Britain that are worthy of a visit (see Appendix B). Some may even be regarded as landmark trees, icons of the highways, byways and waterways of Britain; for example, two magnificent standard trees (together with a smaller, younger example) on the River Cam at Fen Ditton are familiar to Cambridge oarsmen, and are regarded by Rackham as famous trees (Figure 22).[2] Another example, which has been extensively used in black poplar research, is a horizontal tree at Shepreth, fondly known by Cambridge academics as the 'fallen female'.[3] The large urban population in Manchester was familiar to most Mancunians, not so much because of an awareness of the species, but because few other trees were to be found in the area. Perhaps the most amusing story I heard during my years of researching the black poplar was that of Gordon Sharples, of the Local Studies Centre in Manchester. Gordon told me how, as a child, he regularly used to climb the black poplars surrounding the recreation ground in Harpurhey (Figure 23), and get into trouble because of the dangerous spikes on the perimeter fence. However, his *piece de résistance* came just after World War II when he and some friends acquired a French parachute from the local Army and Navy stores, climbed a black poplar in nearby Queen's Park and attempted to parachute out of the top of the tree! The trees in the park conveniently leaned heavily, so there was no likelihood of his efforts being hampered by branches. Perhaps unsurprisingly, the parachute failed to open, but thankfully, Gordon was unharmed and lived to tell his entertaining tale.[4]

Black poplar has evidently grown in the Breckland area of East Anglia for many centuries, in view of the references to timber use in the Middle Ages (see Chapter Two). Today, a group of thirteen magnificent standard trees can be seen around Icklingham (Figure 24), in a habitat very unlike the more usual floodplain situation; the site is a sandy heath, which is now a Site of Special Scientific Interest, due to its abundant flora. According to Rackham, should this landscape be 'multiplied 10,000 times', it would 'evoke the landscape of the Cheyenne Indians', a place where black poplar's close relative, *Populus deltoids*, still grows in woodland and on floodplain. A belt of poplar and elm woodland 300 miles long and half a mile wide fringes the South Platte River, running through Colorado and Nebraska;[5] many of these large American poplar trees echo the rugged splendour of our native black poplar, although to anyone who has seen the puny, nursery-grown specimens of the American species, this may seem difficult to believe.

Rackham regarded black poplar as an abundant tree in the Middle Ages, suggesting that it was the fifth most common non-woodland tree in Suffolk and Essex; he goes as far as to suggest that the lack of black poplar in the modern landscape is the most striking difference between the two periods.[6] However, this does not accord with Evelyn's account of the tree, in which he suggests that it was a rare tree, even in the seventeenth century, and had perhaps always been so.[7] As there is only one mention of *popul* (presumably black poplar) in Anglo-Saxon charters, at Michelmarsh in Hampshire, it seems probable that, had it been as common as Rackham suggests, it would have received more attention.

Rather surprisingly, in view of the number of black poplars to be found in hedgerows, the species has been notably overlooked by a number of authors. Rackham acknowledges their presence, but incorrectly comments that black poplar is not common in hedgerows.[8] I have seen approximately 3,500 trees in total around the British Isles, and the majority of those in rural areas are to be found in hedgerows. The reasons for this are unclear. However, black poplar is particularly easy to propagate, growing well from cuttings and establishing itself quickly. Its prevalence in hedgerows might be taken as an early conservation attempt; concern for the tree's rarity is a distinct possibility, as awareness of the need for tree conservation is not a new concept. Moreover, the tree's landscape impact is evident, as can be seen in the illustrations in this book, and its aesthetic appeal, coupled with its use as a boundary marker, may have encouraged its planting in hedgerows.

FIGURE 22.
The two magnificent landmark trees at Fen Ditton, on the banks of the River Cam, familiar to Cambridge oarsmen.
FIONA COOPER

FIGURE 23.
Row of black poplars between the recreation ground and Conran Street in Harpurhey, Manchester, which Gordon Sharples used to climb as a boy growing up in the 1950s.
FIONA COOPER

FIGURE 24. Landscape view of the unusual habitat surrounding a wonderful population of standard black poplars at Icklingham in Suffolk.
FIONA COOPER

Another puzzle is the geographic imbalance of male and female trees; although the reasons for the paucity of females are reasonably well understood, it is unclear why there are more females in certain counties than others; perhaps the variation is due to differing agricultural and horticultural practices around Britain.

Although many trees are to be found in hedgerows, there is a significant number of trees on common land, on village greens and beside ponds. Herefordshire and Worcestershire are particularly well-provided with commons trees; for example, Checkley Common in Herefordshire has a population of 22 specimens, whilst Castlemorton Common in Worcestershire has around 90 trees, a population which is discussed in greater detail in Chapter Two. Pondside locations appear to be particularly characteristic of the East Anglian population. Although such locations are not truly representative of black poplar's natural habitat, the planting of trees in these situations is an aesthetically pleasing, as well as an ecologically sound, practice: soil conditions around ponds are generally suitable and the practice of planting in such sites could perhaps be regarded as an East Anglian tradition, albeit recent, that should be perpetuated, and utilised throughout the species' range.

Strongholds in Britain

Two areas in Britain contain large numbers of black poplar trees: the Vale of Aylesbury in Buckinghamshire, and Greater Manchester. The Vale of Aylesbury has around 4,500 to 5,000 trees (many of which are unrecorded), whilst Greater Manchester has perhaps 5,000 to 6,000 (all of which are unrecorded), most of which were planted in parks and amenity areas, and which are aged around 80–100 years.[9] These trees are commonly known as 'Manchester poplars', a term which appears to have arisen as a result of the tree's tolerance to smoky air.[10] Numerous examples of black poplar exist in parks, churchyards and other green spaces. There are, however, a number of trees to be found along streamsides, which do not appear to have been planted and may, therefore, be relicts of natural populations, although no females have been confirmed as existing in the city.[11]

Manchester and the North West: a potential catastrophe

It has long been believed amongst tree enthusiasts and ecologists that the Manchester poplar is in some way separate from the remainder of the national population. However, my Ph.D. study, completed in 2001, confirmed that there are no differences in morphology, genetic make-up and invertebrate populations between the poplars around Manchester and those elsewhere in the country. In fact, it was discovered that a tree from Greater Manchester was found to be genetically identical to trees from Ireland, Yorkshire and Sussex. It is therefore evident that this group should not be regarded as a separate entity, but as an important part of the national population, thus potentially almost doubling the number of recorded trees in Britain.

Historically, evidence of poplar populations can be found throughout the North West. For example, there are a number of pubs in this region named The Cotton Tree. These are generally believed to refer to the cotton industry, rather than the presence of female black poplar. However, there is one exception to this assumption, in the village of Cottontree near Colne in Lancashire, where female poplars (hybrid) grow on a streamside. This perhaps calls into the question the association with the cotton industry. However, there is a more serious objection to the idea that these pubs are named for the cotton industry: if that were the case, it would be more logical for pubs to be called either 'The Cotton Mill' or 'The Cotton Field', which are more accurate references to the cotton industry.

The Greater Manchester population is a fascinating piece of industrial history in its own right. The story begins in 1846 with the opening of the first three public parks in Britain, all in the Manchester area: Peel Park, in Salford; Philips Park (originally the grounds of a house); and Queen's Park, in the city of Manchester itself. All were funded by public subscription. At the time the parks were created, industrial pollution had not yet caused damage to trees. When Philips Park was first opened, the area was free from pollution and the park was planted with oak, ash and elm. However, pollution from the increasingly large numbers of industrial plants in the area around the park in the late nineteenth century killed almost all the trees. In 1913, £2,500 was spent restoring the park and replacing the lost trees with black poplar;[12] the species was apparently chosen because of its tolerance to air pollution, combined with the ease with which it could be propagated. Philips Park is now well known for its poplars, and many trees that have died subsequently have been replaced by new cuttings in a restoration project, begun in 2002, as part of the preparations for the Commonwealth Games.[13]

Trees and shrubs for the city were grown at a nursery owned by Manchester Parks and Cemeteries Committee, at Carrington Moss in Cheshire, where some two-thirds of all trees grown were black poplar (around 25,000 in 1915 alone) destined for Manchester.[14] Most of these poplars, which are now approximately 80–90 years old, were planted in streets, parks and amenity areas throughout the city and surrounding areas. No females were planted in the city, because of the problems which could be caused by their fluffy seed, although females can be found in the adjacent counties of Cheshire and Lancashire. The planting was part of a joint project, known as Unemployment Relief Works, between the Government and Manchester Parks and Cemeteries Committee, which was introduced to reduce levels of unemployment in the area.[15] The old head gardener at Philips Park saw the men going out on their pushbikes every day with an iron 'pin' (a small crowbar used to make holes in the ground) and a supply of poplar saplings. The source of the black poplar stock is not clear: Philip Park's head gardener recalled that it was originally drawn from a single tree growing in a disused Lancashire quarry;[16] however, the minutes of the Parks and Cemeteries Committee of Manchester City Council state that trees for Carrington Nursery were purchased from John Hill & Sons, Nurserymen of Stone, Spot Acre Nurseries in Staffordshire, Dickson's Ltd. of Chester and Stephen Treseder & Sons of Cardiff,[17] although no mention is made in the minutes of species supplied by these nurseries.

Other parks in and around Manchester are also well known for the presence of black poplar; for example, Boggart Hole Clough in Blackley has a magnificent avenue of black poplars (Figures 25 and 26) flanking its main thoroughfare. In addition, there is a small row of younger trees on the roadside edge of the park (Figure 27), an increasingly rare sight, as most street and roadside trees have been removed for safety reasons. A park in Gorton is bordered by black poplar that appear to be around 100 years old (Figure 28); sadly, litter in the park suggests that it is a little neglected. Numerous trees are to be found in Heaton Park in Prestwich, particularly in the north-east corner, where younger examples can be seen (Figure 29). Many trees were planted along streets and main roads (Figure 30) but have been removed from the city of Manchester for safety reasons, as noted above, although street trees can still be seen in the Greater Manchester area.

The name 'Manchester poplar' appears to have evolved in the late 1920s and early 1930s; the first written reference to the term was made by Osborn in 1933,[18] (although turn of the century minutes of the Parks and Cemeteries

FIGURE 25.
An avenue of black poplars along the main thoroughfare in Boggart Hole Clough, a lovely park in Blackley, north-west of Manchester. This photograph was taken in the 1950s, when the trees appear to be around 100 years old.
COURTESY OF MANCHESTER LOCAL STUDIES LIBRARY

FIGURE 26.
A more recent view of the thoroughfare in Boggart Hole Clough (see Figure 25), illustrating how little has altered, although some trees have clearly been removed and the remainder are destined for the same fate in the near future, due to the appearance of disease.
FIONA COOPER

FIGURE 27.
Trees along the roadside edge of Boggart Hole Clough; these also show signs of disease, evidenced by the lack of leaves in the crowns.
FIONA COOPER

FIGURE 28.
Black poplars in a park in Gorton, Manchester; black poplars can be seen virtually all around the edge of this park.
FIONA COOPER

Committee of Manchester City Council contain a reference to a request for Mancunian poplar trees for planting at St John's Church, Longsight).[19] Prior to this, the tree was known locally as the 'Blackley poplar', after an area to the north of the city where it may have grown naturally, and which was possibly another source of the cuttings used by the nursery at Carrington. Requests for trees at the turn of the century were infrequent, numbering six in total, so it is evident that species had not yet reached the peak of its popularity. In fact, records show that there were four requests between 1901 and 1905 for elders, by a Rev. T. R. Pennington of Openshaw, who regarded them as 'the only species to flourish in Openshaw'; the repeated request for trees to replace those which had died suggest that the council should perhaps have advised him to plant black poplar, which would not have died as a result of 'smoke and chemics'.[20] However, by the 1930s the minutes of the Parks and Cemeteries Committee contain numerous references to requests for Blackley poplars for amenity planting on roadsides, churchyards and wasteland (Figure 31). These include requests from Moston Colliery, Newton Heath in 1929, from Rev. W. H. Wills of the Manse, Gorton in 1932, and from Whalley Range Cricket and Lawn Tennis Club in 1934.[21]

Tragically, this fascinating population is almost certainly going to be destroyed as a result of disease and the resultant devastation to the landscape cannot be underestimated. Joe Walsh (Arboricultural Officer, Manchester Leisure) was the first to observe young shoots and leaves blackening and dying on black poplars in the area, in the summer of 2000, the wettest year so far on record. The cause was identified as a pathogenic fungus *Venturia populina* (also known as spring defoliation or poplar scab), although this has yet to be confirmed by laboratory analysis. Growth of the fungus is favoured by the greater humidity of recent years, thought to have been brought on by climate change. Only two weeks' wet weather in spring is needed for infection and if this is followed by a hot summer, conditions for the pathogen are ideal. The fungus causes defoliation during the mid-summer period. Following defoliation, infected trees recommence the cycle of leaf growth in late summer, using energy reserves stored for the winter season, and thus enter the winter in a weakened state, which renders them susceptible to further infection. It can, in severe cases, lead to death of the entire tree. To those familiar with the morphology of black poplar, symptoms of *Venturia populina* are relatively easy to spot; initially, the tree's usual dense canopy is much reduced, with many brown leaves visible throughout the tree. New leaves die rapidly, firstly turning black, followed by a brown, shrivelled appearance, which tend to hang onto the tree for longer than is normal at leaf fall time, due to the inability of dead leaves to form an abscission layer at the base of the leaf stalk. The disease also leaves the tree vulnerable to attack by another fungus (*Dothichiza populea*), which, although not as serious, does cause further dieback, particularly in weakened specimens.[22] Trees in the area also appear to be further weakened by rainwater entering fissures between the wood (xylem) and inner bark (phloem), which loosens the bark, causing it to fall off, or be pulled off by destructive children and squirrels.[23] Despite the species' natural resistance to poplar leaf spot, *Marssonnina brunnea*, this is now visible on many trees, presumably due to their weakened state, although it is not thought to be playing a significant role in tree mortality.

By 2002, virtually all trees in the north and east of Manchester were suffering from the disease, but at that stage there were no plans to fell them provided that they did not deteriorate as a result of extensive dieback. It is felt, however, that trees are unlikely to last more than five years. Despite a hot, dry summer in 2003, which is generally thought to be unfavourable for the disease, the problem does not seem to have abated and trees are still rapidly deteriorating, with a number of trees in Heaton Park having fallen. Some 100 trees are due for immediate felling in the park and plans are currently underway to remove all existing trees within the Greater Manchester area, as the disease has moved a further eight miles south between 2002 and 2003.[24] All street trees within the jurisdiction of Manchester City Council had already been removed during the 1970s and 1980s due to the risk of injury from falling branches, and Oldham Metropolitan Borough Council announced in December 2002 that they plan to remove all their black poplars within the next five years, replacing them with a wider variety of species as pollution levels are now much lower and less pollution-tolerant species will therefore survive; however, this will result in the area losing a valuable piece of industrial history. Should the disease continue to spread it is probable that other borough councils throughout the North West will follow with similar action.

The loss of black poplar from the area's landscape will doubtless come as a shock to the inhabitants of Manchester, who have publicly demonstrated their affection for their 'local tree'. In the early 1990s a green space in Hulme, known as Birley fields, was under threat from plans to build a hotel; the redevelopment involved the felling of a 110-year-old poplar known as the Birley Tree, which was thought to be a black poplar. The local pressure group, Hulme Alliance, had tried to obtain a Tree Preservation Order in 1992 and 1994, but were refused on the grounds that the tree was in decline, diseased and hollow. A 24-hour guard was set up at the tree and a fellow of the Arboricultural Association carried out a report, declaring the tree to be an important healthy specimen which would live for at least another 25 years. Sadly these efforts were unsuccessful and the tree was felled during a changeover of guards. However, the tree, perhaps fortunately, was later confirmed as a hybrid species.[25]

I have received several reports of *Venturia populina* in Buckinghamshire and have observed it on trees in the Bledlow area on a recent visit. It also occurs on trees in the Usk valley in south Wales, in Cheshire and in north Staffordshire, suggesting that there is a strong probability of a spread throughout Britain which will almost certainly result in the loss of the national population. Despite this, it has never previously been regarded as a serious disease in Britain – although it is thought to be so in the USA and Italy – and has only been recorded as a problem with young trees in nurseries, where

FIGURE 29.
Young trees which appear to have been planted as a shelterbelt in the north-east corner of Heaton Park in Prestwich. All trees are showing signs of disease.
FIONA COOPER

FIGURE 30.
Young black poplars along a stretch of dual carriageway in Moston, Manchester, once a common sight throughout the city.
COURTESY OF MANCHESTER LOCAL STUDIES LIBRARY

FIGURE 31. Example of black poplar churchyard trees in the north-east of Manchester.
FIONA COOPER

individuals are kept in close proximity. At present, the problem appears to be restricted to black poplar and has not so far affected its close relative, the Lombardy poplar (*P. nigra* var. Italica).

The Vale of Aylesbury

The large, predominantly male (only six females have been confirmed) population in the Vale of Aylesbury is remarkable and has given the landscape a very distinctive and unique appearance. Other than occasional examples of ash and oak, few other species are present, largely as a result of Dutch elm disease, and vast numbers of black poplars are arrayed in neat rows along hedges and streamsides (Figure 32), described by Richard Mabey thus:

> On late afternoons in March, especially when there is a patchy sun glinting from the west, parts of the Vale of Aylesbury in Buckinghamshire are suffused with an exotic orange glow. All over the flood-plain, by dykes and lanes and thin streams, rows of craggy pollards begin to shine, as if they have been coated in amber. Closer to, the sprays of twigs seem kaleidoscopic. They have ochre bark, ginger-shellacked buds, and the germs of what will soon be voluptuous crimson catkins.[26]

As he rightly states, 'this spectacular display of the largest concentration of our grandest native tree' is unique to the Vale of Aylesbury. However, the population, despite extensive survey by Alan Holmes, and meticulous recording and mapping in recent years, is something of a mystery. Little documentary evidence has been found relating to it, despite extensive searches in the British Library by Alan Holmes and Lesley Davies, and preliminary research by myself into estate records held at the Buckinghamshire County Records Office. As some 60 per cent of the population is pollard examples (Figure 33), one would imagine that there had been a significant need for the timber in some form of industry. However, the only reference to such a use is made by William Page in *The Victoria History of the County of Buckingham*, who states that black poplar timber may have been utilised for the construction of buffers for railway goods wagons, which were 'found to bear concussion better'.[27] There was a large railway carriage works at Wolverton in the north of the county, but the hedges containing many of the trees in the Vale post-date the rather short-lived use of timber in the industry. The other use of poplar timber (species unspecified) in railway carriage construction was for brake-blocks,[28] but again this was short-lived; once locomotives became faster in the mid to late nineteenth century, cast iron blocks were used.[29] The only other reference to poplar timber in the area is made by Rose, who suggests that any form of timber use was quite unlikely; a carpenter living in Haddenham wrote, probably in the early 1930s, that there was 'no use for poplar, this went to Chesham for bush and broom making'.[30]

We are thus left to speculate on the origins of the population; several possibilities come to mind. Black poplars may have been planted in the Vale as boundary markers for local estates at the time of the Enclosure Acts in the eighteenth century, the species being chosen because of its ability to survive in wet areas, which were prevalent around Aylesbury.[31] The population would have the added benefit of reducing soil moisture, thus reducing the need for land drainage operations. Another possibility is that timber was utilised in the paper industries in the south of the county,[32] after the use of rags was abandoned; black poplar would have been a very suitable substitute, being a comparatively soft timber suitable for pulping. Hybrid poplar is still used in the paper industry today. Alternatively, it is possible that black poplar pollards were used until the Second World War to provide poles for making sheep hurdles (rather in the way that hazel was used in Dorset) with which to construct sheepfolds in the Vale during winter months.[33]There is also the possibility that black poplar was chosen as it was already known to be an endangered species, and that the person responsible for the planting was perhaps an early, anonymous enthusiast, although this would have required the cooperation of a great many landowners.

In view of the densely packed nature of the population in the Vale of Aylesbury (in an area to the north of the town, one square kilometre alone holds 105 trees), these trees are at particular risk from *Venturia populina*, which has already been observed in the north of the county in 2003[34] and by myself in 2004.

Following Alan Holmes' baseline study around Aylesbury in the 1990s, when all poplars in the area looked after by Aylesbury Vale District Council

Countryside Project were surveyed and mapped, a follow-up study of six one-kilometre grid squares was recently carried out. There was an average of 8.9 per cent loss of trees from these squares since the original survey. This is due to a number of factors, such as the occasional unexplained disappearance of trees (possibly as a result of removal by landowners), wind-throw (Figure 34) and, in many cases, the death of trees following extensive pollarding after a long period of neglect.[35] The last cause is a phenomenon that I have seen frequently around Britain, always following a similar pattern, with newly pollarded trees frequently displaying vigorous growth for several months before dying; such drastic trimming is obviously a form of physiological stress that they are unable to tolerate. The death of new pollards in the Vale of Aylesbury was originally thought to be the result of pollarding during periods of low rainfall, but as trees on streamsides have also died following pollarding it is now believed that hydrological factors are not a contributory cause, although this is not yet certain. Further research into the phenomenon is clearly necessary, as it appears to be a separate issue to that which is currently facing forest pathologists, who are engaged in research into the fungal pathogen problem.

FIGURE 32.
Black poplars alongside a stream in the Vale of Aylesbury.
FIONA COOPER

FIGURE 33.
A neglected pollard in the Vale of Aylesbury. If left alone, it is probable that down-sweeping branches will embed themselves into the ground and ensure the tree's survival for many more years.
FIONA COOPER

FIGURE 34.
Wind-thrown black poplar in the Vale of Aylesbury. Unfortunately this tree looks unlikely to regenerate.
FIONA COOPER

CHAPTER FOUR

Black Poplar Population Surveys

Introduction

The current surge of interest in black poplar and its distribution in Britain was largely as a result of the work of Edgar Milne-Redhead, who, as described above (Chapter One), undertook a national survey between 1973 and 1988 on behalf of the Botanical Society of the British Isles (BSBI) and the World Wildlife Fund (WWF) to establish the number of remaining trees in England and Wales.[1] He established that only around 1,000 trees remained. However, his enthusiasm ensured that the species was not forgotten, and we owe to Edgar's early work and enthusiasm our current knowledge of the species' distribution, which is perhaps greater than it has ever been.

Historical distribution of black poplar in the British Isles

A study of old county floras and historical timber references indicates that considerable disagreement exists regarding the native status of black poplar and the distribution of the species throughout Britain, much of which was due to confusion between black poplar and hybrid species, which has resulted in considerable incorrect recording of the tree's distribution.[2] Historical data obtained from county floras suggest that the distribution range of black poplar is restricted to England and Wales, south of the Lune and Humber estuaries, with a few isolated examples in Cumbria, Northumbria, west Wales and Cornwall. However, it was believed by many authors to be an alien, perhaps because it has been extensively planted, particularly in hedgerows, coupled with the fact that little or no natural regeneration has taken place. The following paragraphs describe the regional distribution as it was known prior to comparatively recent surveys.

Southern England

Accounts of black poplar distribution and frequency in this region vary between writer and county. In his *Flora of Guernsey and the Lesser Channel Islands*, Marquand reported that the tree was 'frequent, but planted'. He did not put forward any suggestions as to its arrival on the Channel Islands, nor make comment on its relationship to European or British black poplars.[3] The species is still found in the Channel Islands, and is currently thought to be the same subspecies as exists in mainland Britain.[4] In Cornwall, Paton reported that black poplar is sometimes planted in woods, parks, along roadsides and in damp valleys,[5] but he may have been confusing the species with hybrid poplars, as only two trees are currently recorded in the county, both of which are planted individuals. Further east, Keble-Martin noted that the first record of the species in Devon was made in 1797, and regarded it as an alien that was found near streams and other wet places. He mentions nineteen records and comments on the presence of a few individual trees in Somerset, Devon and Cornwall.[6] In *The Flora of Dorsetshire*, Mansell Pleydell considers the tree to be native, with a general distribution by rivers and in damp woods. He mentions that it is found in Devon, Hampshire and Somerset, and Normandy in France.[7] His feeling was that the tree was naturalised, but non-indigenous in Hampshire, where it was found on damp ground and by rivers. Townsend describes it as a 'fluviatile tree' and reports that it was first recorded in 1849.[8] Interestingly, Milne-Redhead mentions plentiful pollarded black poplars on the Somerset Levels,[9] although no other reference has yet been found regarding these trees, and I did not observe any during my Ph.D. fieldwork. White, writing about the flora of Bristol, lists the tree as 'rather rare' and notes that it was found in woodland and swampy ground around the city, but does not comment on its native status.[10] To the east, in Wiltshire, Grose discusses the presence of both *P. nigra* subsp *nigra* and *P. nigra* subsp *betulifolia*. He regarded the former as an alien and the latter as probably native. Only females of the former subspecies were known, and only males of the latter; both were listed as rare and to be found on riverbanks, marshes and other damp places.[11] However, as no current records of *P. nigra* subsp *nigra* exist anywhere in Britain, it is possible that Grose was confusing the two sub-species, possibly due to slight morphological differences between the sexes (wherein the female frequently has more slender twigs). To the north of the region, Riddelsdell *et al.* record *P. nigra* var *viridis* rather than subsp *betulifolia* as native in Gloucestershire and suggest that it was generally distributed and 'frequent in the Vale';[12] they were presumably referring to the vale of the River Severn (Figures 35 and 36). Two county floras for Sussex give conflicting reports of the tree's presence in the county. Arnold states that it was a very common tree, planted in woods and on roadsides, and that the species was first recorded in 1897.[13] However, Wolley-Dod reports that black poplar was unknown in Sussex.[14] As the tree is still found in this county, and the population is predominantly female, it is possible that the former author may have included hybrid species, and that the latter author was perhaps a little unobservant. Hanbury and Marshall report the tree as 'not uncommon in Kent'[15] but possibly as a result of confusion with hybrids, as there are now only 26 trees in Kent listed on the national register. Salmon, writing on Surrey, refers to 38 individuals of both sexes between Putney and Barnes by the River Thames, which remain today, and are probably a remnant wild population (Figure 37). He regarded the tree as not uncommon and dates the first record to 1852, at Putney.[16] In Hertfordshire, Cook's *Manners of Raising and Ordering Fruit Trees*

FIGURE 35.
A magnificent standard black poplar, and probably one of the country's largest, adjacent to what is reputed to be the longest village green in England at Frampton-on-Severn, Gloucestershire.
FIONA COOPER

FIGURE 36.
Superb old pollard that appears to have been the inspiration for the name of the House in Tree pub, near Staverton in Gloucestershire.
FIONA COOPER

FIGURE 37.
Row of male and female trees along the south bank of the River Thames between Hammersmith and Putney bridges, which may be a relict population.
FIONA COOPER

HOUSE IN
THE TREE

records that black poplar 'grows in several places about Ware';[17] Little, in his article on 'Hertfordshire poplars' notes several trees in the county, but does not believe the tree to be common.[18] Black poplar was first recorded in Middlesex in 1737 and, according to Trimen, is a rare tree of riverbanks and damp places.[19] However, Kent, writing about the same county, maintains that the tree was first recorded in 1638, although he, like Trimen, regarded the tree as rare and to be found in hedgerows and along streamsides.[20]

The heart of England

Druce suggests in his floras of Oxfordshire,[21] Northamptonshire[22] and Buckinghamshire[23] that the tree is a 'rare, sylvestral, localised alien denizen', found in hedges and plantations. However, he goes on to quote Elwes, who regarded the tree as native to the Welsh Border. Druce was also of the opinion that the tree is a 'conspicuous feature in the scenery of the Thames and Kennet valleys'.[24] He gives five records for Northamptonshire[25] and, rather surprisingly, he regarded it as 'very local and rare' in Buckinghamshire,[26] despite the large population around Aylesbury (Figure 38). In addition, Reed makes no mention of the tree in his book on the Buckinghamshire landscape.[27] Dony stated that the tree is 'frequent by large rivers in Bedfordshire', and that it is recorded for all neighbouring counties;[28] however, only 60 trees are currently recorded in the county.

East Anglia

In this region, black poplar was generally considered to be common. In Suffolk, Hind reported black poplar as frequent, and generally planted on riverbanks and hedges (Figure 39), where the first tree was recorded in 1773.[29] Simpson regarded the tree as native and generally rare throughout the county, but formerly more frequent.[30] Petch and Swann, writing about Norfolk, regarded it as native and frequent, usually by streamsides.[31] The oldest recorded tree still standing is in this county, at West Harling, and was originally recorded by Sir Thomas Browne, in a communication to John Evelyn, in 1663.[32] In Cambridgeshire, to the west of this region, Babington records the tree as *P. nigra officinarum* and says it is plentiful in wetland, a habitat with which the county is well provided, and by water.[33]

Midlands

Lees wrote of Worcestershire that 'a few scraggy black poplars (*P. nigra)* appear in various localities by brooksides', but rather incorrectly suggested that this tree appeared to be dying out; some 500 trees are now recorded on the national register in the county, most of which are around 200 years old.[34] Bagnall regarded the tree as a rare alien in Warwickshire, where it was found on riverbanks.[35] Further north, in the south and west of Staffordshire, it was found by streams and roadsides (Figure 40), reflecting its current distribution.[36] Leighton, writing on Shropshire, stated that it was present on the banks of the Teme in the south of the county, and in a few sites around what is now

Telford;[37] however, with a current population of around 300 mature trees, particularly in south-west Shropshire, it is probable that he under-recorded trees. Sinker *et al.*, describing the same county, noted that black poplar was a tree of hedgerows, pond margins, and also occurred as isolated specimens on moist to moderately dry soils. It was apparently native on the flood-plain of the River Severn and tributaries, where it often occurred as an isolated tree, the remains of former woodland, and it was occasionally planted in hedges from local native stock (Figure 41). However, it was scarce in the north of the county.[38] In Leicestershire and Rutland the tree appears to have been uncommon: Primavesi and Evans give only one record in the county, at Barlestone;[39] Hawood and Neol regarded it as 'occasional' and give four records;[40] whilst Messenger does not include the species in his *Flora of Rutland*.[41] In the extreme north of the region, accounts are slightly contradictory. Linton says it is a frequent alien in Derbyshire, found in hedges and plantations, and on riversides.[42] However, Clapham does not include it in his *flora* of the same county, a surprising omission given the large population of some 200 mature trees in the Dove valley, south-west of Derby.[43] Opinions conflict in Nottinghamshire, with Howitt describing black poplar as 'rather frequent in wet places',[44] whilst Howitt and Howitt describe it as a 'rather rare native or denizen'.[45]

Yorkshire and the North East

In his *Flora of Lincolnshire*, Gibbons suggested that black poplar was native in Stapleford but planted elsewhere in the county[46] but, intriguingly, he does not elaborate upon this. Further north, in Yorkshire, Robinson states that the tree is an alien in east Yorkshire, and that it is frequent around Hull,[47] but he may have confused it with the hybrid species as no trees are currently recorded in this area. The tree was regarded by Lees, in west Yorkshire, as an alien, and it was always planted in hedges and plantations.[48] Sykes, writing more recently, reported that a number of trees in north Yorkshire had been recorded as black poplar, but felt that they had been confused with hybrid species, as none were found within National Park boundaries during 'the recent survey'.[49] Winch and Thornhill stated that *P. nigra* could be found 'on the banks of rivers' in Northumberland and Co. Durham, but did not give any precise locations.[50] Swan described the tree as an alien of Northumberland, planted in Embleton, Howick, Alnwick and Hulse Park, but regarded it as native south of the Mersey and Humber estuaries and, perhaps somewhat illogically, as formerly native in Co. Durham.[51] In his guide to the flora of the post-1974 county of Cleveland, Lawrence discusses black poplar types, but makes no specific mention of the planted examples of the tree in Middlesborough.[52] Graham regarded the species as 'introduced, formerly native' in Co. Durham and gives seven records, which were apparently considered by Edgar Milne-Redhead to have been derived from local stock,[53] although such a view seems to contradict Milne-Redhead's belief that the black poplar's native range was south of an imaginary line between the Mersey and Humber estuaries.

FIGURE 38.
A contender for one of the largest trees in the Vale of Aylesbury, displaying the characteristic lean; sadly the tree is hollow and therefore vulnerable to wind-throw.
FIONA COOPER

FIGURE 39.
Pondside black poplar at Campsea Ashe in Suffolk, which has fallen and regenerated.
FIONA COOPER

FIGURE 40.
Fallen black poplar on a damp ditch-bank at Albrighton, on the county boundary between Shropshire and Staffordshire, which has regenerated to produce a multi-stemmed tree.
KATE PAYNE

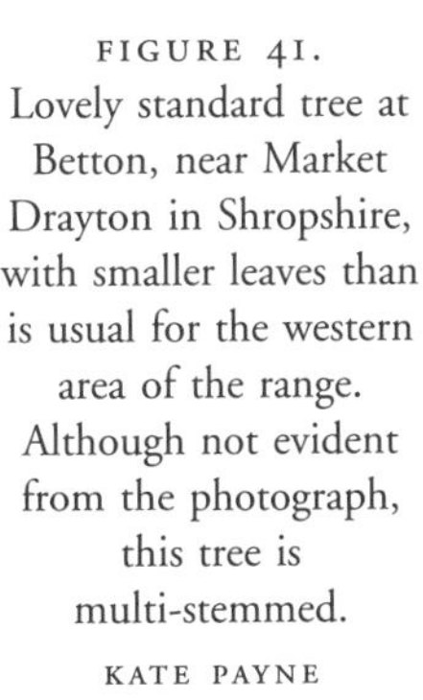

FIGURE 41.
Lovely standard tree at Betton, near Market Drayton in Shropshire, with smaller leaves than is usual for the western area of the range. Although not evident from the photograph, this tree is multi-stemmed.
KATE PAYNE

The North West

In south Lancashire, black poplar was regarded by Travis as introduced and naturalised, and was apparently found in hedges, plantations and woods.[54] Wheldon and Wilson concur, stating that the species was a frequently planted alien in west Lancashire, and the first recorded example was located on the Leck Beck.[55] Halliday lists only one tree, by the River Eden, and incorrectly states that this tree is the most northerly recorded example (see Chapter One) (Figure 42).[56]

Wales

Ellis, in his book *Aliens in the British Flora*, describes the tree as an established alien in the Principality, and says it is found in hedgerows in the counties of Monmouth, Glamorgan, Brecon, Montgomeryshire, Merionithshire, Denbigh, Flint, Caernarvonshire and Anglesey.[57] Wade *et al.* regard it as introduced and frequently planted in Glamorgan,[58] but no mention is made of black poplar by Hyde and Wade in *Welsh Flowering Plants*,[59] perhaps due to a general lack of awareness of the species' identification and distribution prior to 1973. Rather surprisingly, no mention is made of the significant population in the Usk Valley in Breconshire, which comprises some of the best examples of black poplar in the west of the range (Figure 43). Perhaps most importantly, Britain's largest tree is to be found in Brecon, a magnificent standard used as a boundary marker near the river in the grounds of Christ College (Figure 44).

The Republic of Ireland

In his *An Irish Flora*, Webb states that the tree was occasionally planted in the south of Ireland, suggesting he did not regard it as a native species.[60] The anonymous *Cybele Hibernica*, of 1899, records the tree as frequent in Ireland, but always planted near houses,[61] also suggesting that human intervention may have been responsible for its presence in Ireland. The majority of trees in Ireland are found in the Irish Midlands, particularly in the Shannon, Barrow and Liffey river valleys, with a concentration of trees in hedgerows to the west of Dublin in Co. Kildare. However, Hobson, in his book *The black poplar in Ireland: its distribution and origin*, conflicts directly with the views expressed in *Cybele Hibernica*. He found no correlation between the presence of black poplars and human settlement and felt that many trees originated naturally, concluding that the tree is a native Irish species. As Hobson's fieldwork took place in August, he was not able to ascertain the number of female trees in Ireland (seed is shed in June, and catkins and seeds are the only indication of sex of trees). However, Hobson suspected natural regeneration at a site on the shores of Lough Ree, indicating the presence of one or more females. He also found a tree in Enniscorthy, Co. Wexford, adjacent to the Cotton Tree Bar, which he thought to be female in view of the name of the bar (see Chapter Three).[62] Another argument for native status in Ireland is the presence of bossed and unbossed trees. Most bossed trees are found in the east of the country, with the exception of some obviously planted, isolated individuals in the south and west. It is possible that these specimens that may have been brought from Britain, whilst the bossless trees are native to Ireland. Although unbossed trees exist in Britain, they are quite unlike the ones observed in Ireland, which are found mainly in the west of the range.

Recent black poplar survey work

During the latter part of the 1990s, interest in black poplar increased dramatically, with surveys conducted at both local and national levels. Estimates of the number of trees present prior to the commencement of this study have varied according to the author consulted. Both Tabbush and Rogers reported that approximately 2,000 individuals remained.[63] However, Mabey suggested that this figure should be in the region of 6,000,[64] in order to take into account the large population of unrecorded trees in the Vale of Aylesbury. As part of my Ph.D., I needed to collect leaf material from trees for the genetic aspect of the study. While collecting this material, I was able to conduct a partial survey of each county in order to endeavour to bring the national record up to date. As fieldwork was carried out in early summer, I was also able to ascertain the sex of a number of trees and thus obtain a more accurate estimate of the female population.

A number of local surveys had taken place throughout the British Isles and Ireland, prior to the commencement of my research. These have greatly assisted in expanding our knowledge of the tree's current status. Leeds Groundwork Trust has located and recorded some twenty trees;[65] Lancashire County Council has conducted similar work[66] and the Forestry Commission has surveyed Clwyd.[67] The Environment Agency surveyed Montgomeryshire, Shropshire, Worcestershire and the western fringe of Staffordshire during their genetic study in 1996.[68] Other counties that have been extensively surveyed are: Somerset;[69] Sussex;[70] Middlesex;[71] Essex;[72] Buckinghamshire;[73] Warwickshire;[74] Suffolk;[75] Leicestershire;[76] Derbyshire;[77] Norfolk;[78] Brecon;[79] Monmouth;[80] Clwyd;[81] Cheshire;[82] Cambridgeshire;[83] Huntingdonshire;[84] Nottinghamshire;[85] Yorkshire;[86] Lancashire;[87] and Wiltshire.[88] Findings from these surveys have not been published, although the organisations involved have very kindly passed their results on to me, enabling me to add them to the national register of trees.

Despite the suggestion made by Elwes and Henry that the tree was rare in Gloucestershire,[89] a survey by Sonia Holland found nearly 360 trees, of which 77 were confirmed as female.[90] A survey of Herefordshire was undertaken by Watkins *et al.*, who found 170 trees, many of which were previously unrecorded.[91] Ongoing surveys are being conducted in Cheshire,[92] Sussex[93] and the North East (Northumbria, Tyne and Wear and County Durham).[94] An intensive survey was carried in Derbyshire by Derbyshire Wildlife Trust, in which I took part by verifying samples from photographs and twigs, sent to me by post (Figure 45).

In August 1997, prior to commencement of this study, I was, to my

FIGURE 42.
Female roadside tree near Nantwich, in Cheshire.
FIONA COOPER

FIGURE 43. Example of a magnificent black poplar, used as an ornamental tree in the grounds of Nevill Hall Hospital at Abergavenny, in Monmouthshire. The area has some of the best examples of standard trees in Britain

FIONA COOPER

immense pride, appointed black poplar National Recorder and Referee for the Botanical Society of the British Isles. This voluntary work is carried out in conjunction with the Biological Records Centre (BRC) and involves the collation of records of new finds, losses and sex identification from individuals and groups throughout the country, in order to maintain the national record. It also involves identification of trees from twigs, descriptions and photographs submitted by recorders and interested groups such as wildlife trusts and local councils. The record consists of a grid reference, Vice County (VC) number (VC is the division of the country into areas which approximately equate to the pre-1974 county boundaries),[95] the name of the recorder, the number and sex of trees (where the latter is known) and a brief site name.

The field survey that was conducted as part of my study and the collation of data from other individuals and groups has dramatically increased our knowledge regarding the distribution and numbers of trees in Britain. The total number of recorded trees has increased from around 2,500 to around 7,000, and numbers of confirmed females has increased from 150 to 600 (Figure 46). Recording of pollarded trees was not undertaken prior to my study, and this new information has identified those areas where timber utilisation was likely to have been more intense. Such data will be of value to groups wishing to implement clone banks or planting programmes. The survey work undertaken by this and other more localised studies has clarified the confusion over the distribution and identity of the species throughout Britain and Ireland. The presence of trees, both male and female, in riverside locations as far north as Lancashire and Yorkshire indicate that the probable native range of the tree is more northerly than previously supposed.

Morphological differences

In Britain, the tree appears to have three distinct leaf morphologies, with a clear geographical distribution. Such differentiation has resulted in an unofficial sub-taxonomy being devised by John White, formerly dendrologist for the Forestry Commission at Westonbirt Arboretum. He suggests the following forms: 'large-leafed St Asaph type', found in the west of the range; 'diamond-leafed Rossendale type', found in the north; and the 'Cambridge type', found in the east, and thought to represent the best leaf form of black poplar.[96] There are several explanations of the variations. First, it is possible that sub-sub-species exist, or that more than one sub-species is present. Second, the variation may reflect the existence of several ecotypes (the adaptation of a species to environmental conditions). Third, the variation may be due to environmental influences, such as microclimate or altitude, although this latter possibility appears to be less likely as a tree grown from a cutting in a different locality retained the characteristics of the parent tree.[97] Personal observation during fieldwork has indicated that, in addition to variation in leaf morphology, great variation in bark also occurs. Most trees in Britain have bark of a dark brown colour. However, trees in Somerset frequently have pale grey bark, whilst trees in the Vale of Aylesbury and Oxfordshire have a lighter brown bark. In addition to this variation, sexual dimorphism exists between male and female trees, with female trees displaying more slender twigs than male trees, particularly in the north of the range. Fissuring and bossing can also vary, with some trees in the Republic of Ireland, Cheshire and Gloucestershire having no bosses at all.

The distribution of black poplar pollards

The distribution of pollarded black poplars varies greatly. Despite Rackham's statement that pollards are rarely found outside East Anglia,[98] there are numerous examples throughout Britain, particularly in Buckinghamshire, Derbyshire, Herefordshire, Worcestershire and East Anglia. All confirmed pollarded specimens in Britain are illustrated on the dot map (Figure 47). It is unclear why Shropshire has only six pollard black poplars, as a number of houses around Acton Scott, near Church Stretton in Shropshire, are reputedly constructed of black poplar timber[99] and these houses are *not* cruck-framed, a building method for which the black poplar standard is especially well suited. No pollard trees have been recorded in Cheshire, Lancashire or Cumbria, nor in the Republic of Ireland, supporting Hobson's view that the tree was not associated with human settlement or timber utilisation in Ireland.

Male and female distribution

Until recently, the female black poplar was regarded as extremely rare. Prior to the mid-1990s, it was believed that only 150 existed in Britain[100] but this was probably due to under-recording generally, or surveys being undertaken at the wrong time of year for gender identification. Accordingly, Rackham states that the 'female black poplar is very rare indeed'.[101] Curiously, the distribution of females is uneven, with strong concentrations in Dorset, Gloucestershire, Oxfordshire, Cheshire, Sussex and East Anglia; the reasons for this are unclear. The most northerly confirmed female is in County Durham, an area not generally regarded as within the tree's native range.[102] Taking into consideration the unpopularity of females, it is unlikely that a female would have been transported over a large distance for planting purposes, when a more local, male tree could have been used, adding weight to the argument that the species' native range is more northerly than previously believed.

FIGURE 44.
The largest (by girth) recorded black poplar in Britain, at Brecon in Powys. The tree is 31.5 metres tall and has a girth of 6.85 metres at 1.3 metres from the ground.
FIONA COOPER

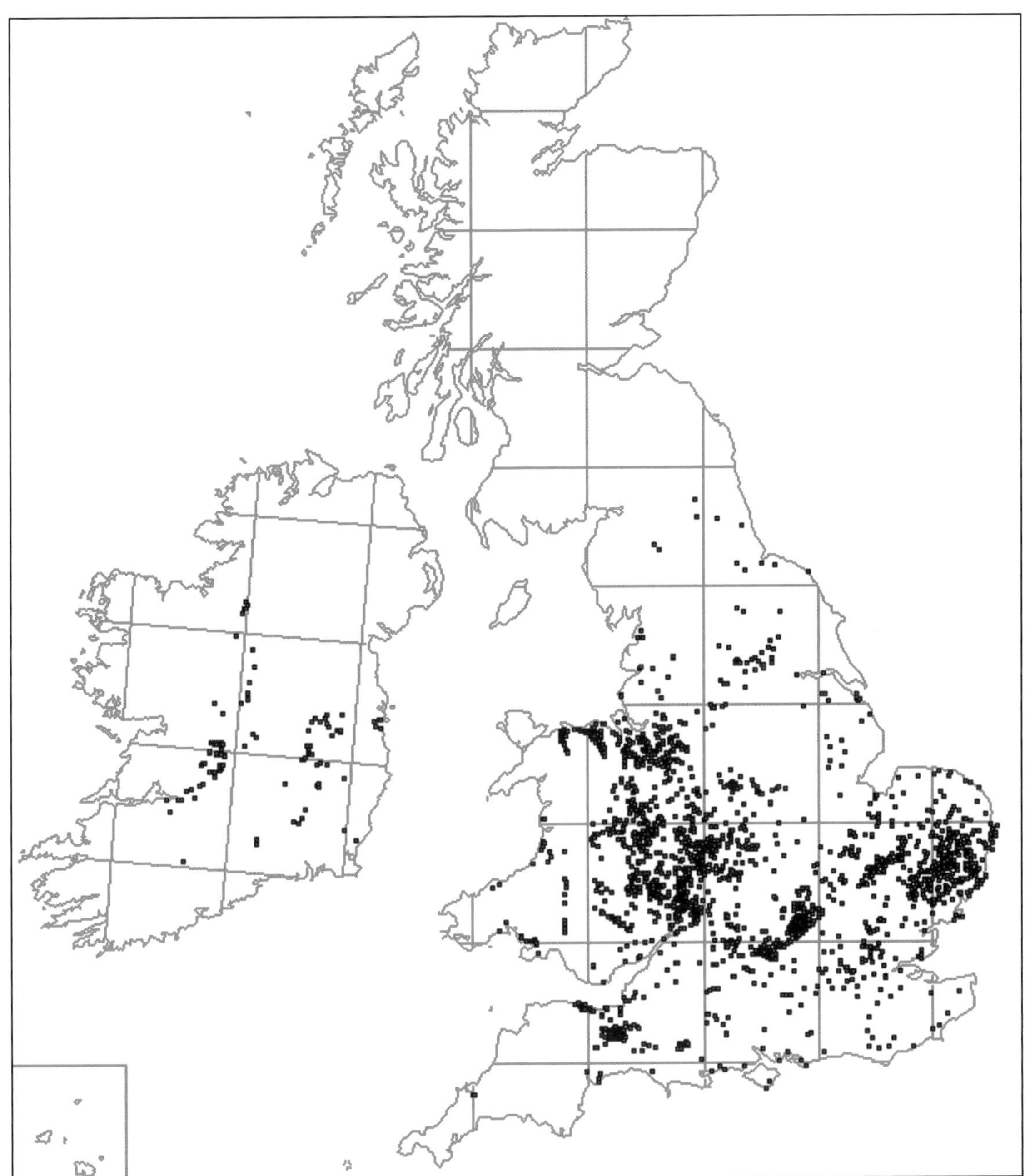

FIGURE 45.
Distribution map of all recorded black poplars in Britain and Ireland.
SCENESETTERS

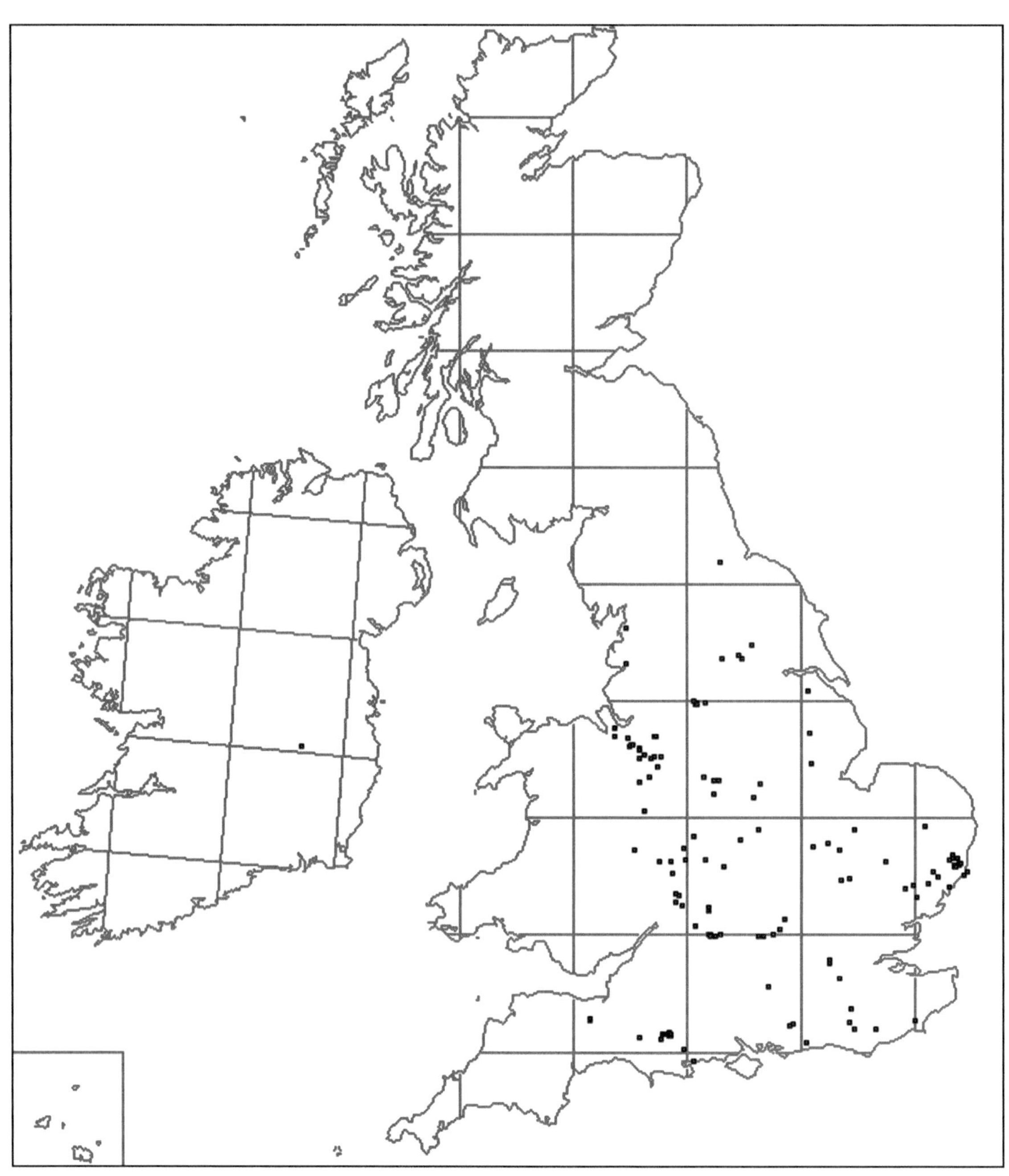

FIGURE 46.
Distribution map of all confirmed female black poplars in Britain and Ireland.
SCENESETTERS

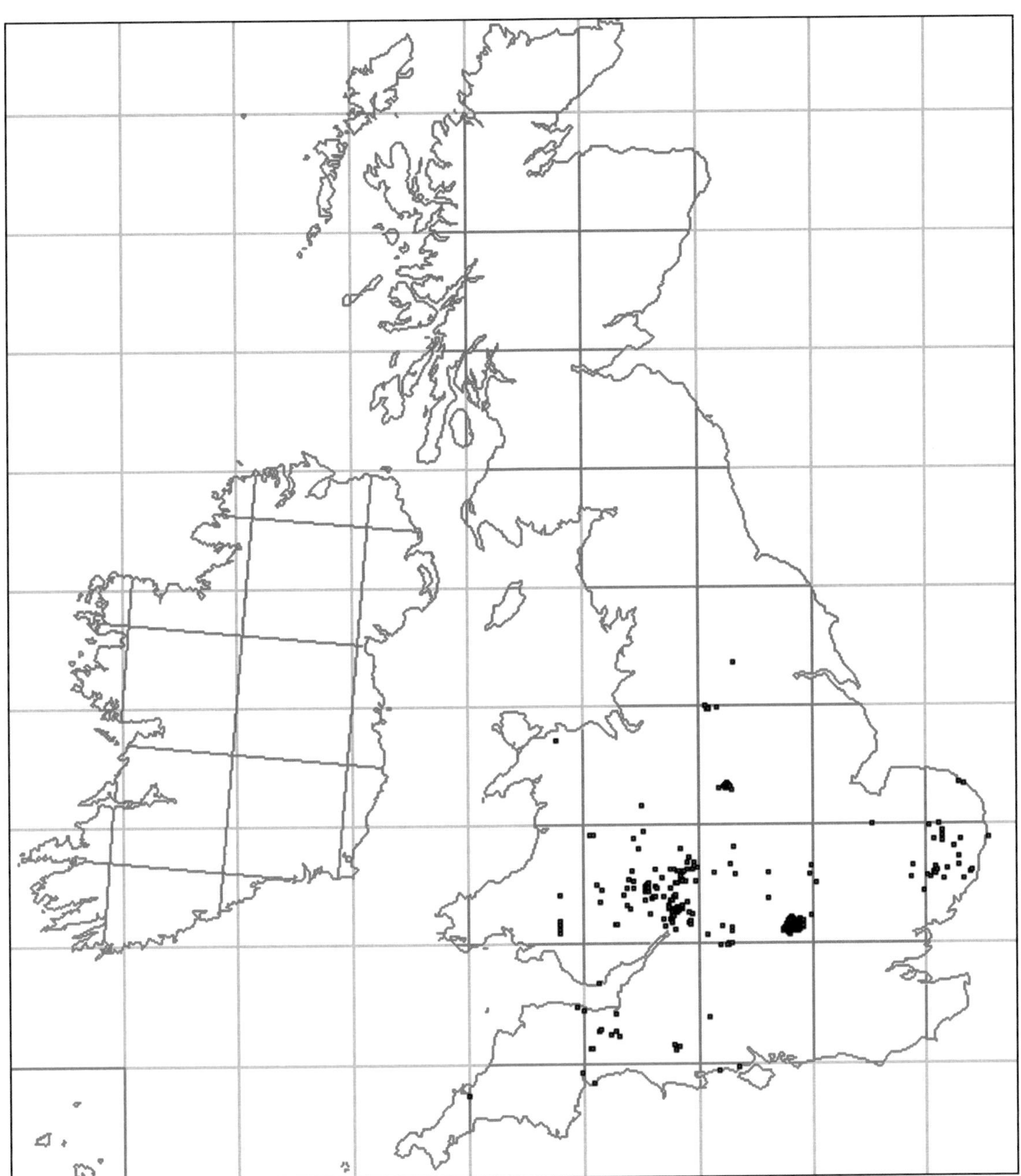

FIGURE 47.
Distribution map of all recorded black poplar pollards in Britain and Ireland.
SCENESETTERS

CHAPTER FIVE

Genetic Analysis of the Black Poplar

Introduction

Included here is a brief review of work that has been carried out on genetic diversity in woody species, as it is relevant to the plight of black poplar, a tree that displays high levels of similarity, thus rendering it prone to destruction by disease. Genetic analysis can be a useful tool in conservation programmes, since it can measure levels of genetic diversity within species and establish genetic relatedness within or between species, to enable comparisons of similarity to be made. Genetic analysis can also be usefully employed to establish where hybrid introgression has occurred. Hybrid introgression occurs by repeated backcrossing of a hybrid to one or both parents. Brown feels that hybridisation is only of concern when it has arisen from anthropomorphic activity,[1] such as that which is believed to have occurred with the *Populus* genus.[2] Genetic analysis is often the only method of distinguishing whether introgression has taken place in a particular tree, since it cannot always be determined in the field using phenotypic characteristics.[3]

Authors on the topic have suggested that genetic diversity is important to conservation in various ways. The loss of genetic diversity reduces species' evolutionary potential; additionally, high genetic variation is positively related to species' fitness. In both of these cases, loss of genetic diversity can lead to a decrease in an organism's ability to respond to environmental changes[4] and other destructive forces, such as disease. Moreover, it must not be forgotten that genetic diversity can interact with three groups of factors: abiotic forces, such as soil, climate and location; biotic factors, such as competition, symbiosis, parasitism and predation; and population size, mating, mutation, migration and dispersal. In transplant experiments between populations, for example, introduced plants appeared to be around 50 per cent less fit than the native plants.[5]

The devastation that low genetic diversity can cause was illustrated in America by the corn blight which occurred in 1970, when the vast majority of a crop of inbred maize was destroyed. The following year the crop was modified with blight resistant genes from wild Mexican maize in order to prevent future devastation caused by reliance on a narrow genetic base.[6]

Between the sixteenth and twentieth centuries, losses to the *Solanum* (potato) gene pool occurred due to selective breeding and viruses, with little genetic variation being added to the gene pool.[7] The well-known potato famine that occurred in Ireland in the nineteenth century was due to an attack by the fungal pathogen, *Phytophthora* spores, on crops with a narrow genetic base.[8]

The primary conclusion from two decades of plant population genetics research is that different species vary greatly in their level of genetic diversity.[9] As a result, consideration needs to be given to the genetic analysis of groups of plants. For example, the *Pinus* genus, because of its economic importance, has undergone extensive analysis for genetic variation. However, little work has been undertaken to study genetic variation in temperate broad-leaved species other than the *Populus* genus, making comparisons between my study and other species somewhat difficult.

The importance of genetic diversity

Whilst few extinctions are thought to have occurred as a result of low genetic diversity, it remains an important consideration in view of the risk posed by new diseases or anthropogenic activity. An example is provided by the American chestnut (*Castanea dentata* Mill), which had a geographic distribution from New England to Alabama and accounted for 40 per cent of overstorey canopy in forests.[10] It was an important timber tree and supported a 'wide variety of wildlife'.[11] However, it fell victim to a fungal attack (*Endothia parasitica* Murr) in 1904, affecting the above-ground portions of the tree, but not the roots, resulting in death of the shoots when they reach 'a few centimetres in diameter', thus considerably reducing the economic value of this tree. Hamrick and Godt suggest that the devastating effect upon the tree arose as a result of a lack of genetic diversity,[12] although the authors do not comment on the level of diversity found. However, a study by Huang *et al.* to establish genetic diversity in wild populations of American chestnut indicated that heterozygosity levels varied between 0.196 and 0.096, giving an average of 0.146, equating to 14.5 per cent variation. The authors felt this result reflected a low level of genetic diversity, and that this was a contributory factor in the decline of the tree,[13] supporting Hamrick and Godt's suggestion that high genetic variability is essential for species' survival.

'Rare species' are defined by Hamrick and Godt thus: 'although not presently threatened with extinction, [the species] is in such small numbers throughout its range that it may become endangered if its present environment worsens'.[14] The definition of 'endangered species' is given by Holsinger and Gottlieb as those whose 'prospects of survival and reproduction are in immediate jeopardy from one or more causes'.[15] Whilst endangered species are generally rare, rare species are not necessarily endangered, as rarity may be characteristic for a species. Rarity may be of concern, however, if it results from anthropogenic influence.[16]

Genetic analysis of woody species

Although literature regarding molecular studies of tree species exists, it is by no means common, and the majority of studies that do exist have been conducted on gymnosperms, such as the *Pinus* genus, primarily due, as noted above, to its economic importance.[17] As my study was not concerned with gymnosperms, the following paragraphs focus upon hardwood angiosperms. Studies reviewed have employed a range of molecular techniques.

Muluvi *et al.* investigated the level of genetic variation in *Moringa oleifera,* an important African multi-purpose timber tree introduced from India. Populations from Kenya, Southern Malawi and South India were sampled, and it was found that 59.15 per cent of variability existed as variation between all populations, whilst 18.59 per cent of variability existed between African and Indian populations. The highest levels of genetic diversity (44.53 per cent) were found within the Indian populations, whilst the less widely dispersed Kenyan populations had the lowest levels of diversity (14.44 per cent). The authors suggested that these varying levels of diversity resulted from selection pressure by cultivators in populations that were based on a small initial number of trees from India.[18]

Rossetto *et al.* found that samples of *Grevillea scapigera,* an endangered Australian woody shrub, were 75 per cent similar, and that most variation existed between individuals rather than between populations. They felt that this result indicated a high level of diversity for an endangered species.[19]

Wachira *et al.* studied genetic diversity in 38 tea (*Camellia sinensis*) individuals, and found that similarity ranged from 43 per cent to 96 per cent. Although the tree was thought to have been introduced from individuals in a geographically restricted area (from the Assam region in south-east Asia to Kenya), most variability (93.6 per cent) was found within populations from these sources. Wachira *et al.* found that 70 per cent of variability was within populations while 30 per cent was between populations,[20] which is in agreement with a previous study, where it was found that outbreeding woody plants retain considerable variability, particularly within populations.[21] The findings from the study were supported by the findings of Paul *et al.*, who studied diversity in Indian and Kenyan tea (*Camellia sinensis* (L.) O. Kuntze) and found that most diversity (79 per cent) was detected within, rather than between, populations.[22]

Byrne and Moran studied genetic variation in 10 *Eucalyptus nitens* individuals, a tree native to Australia, with a natural distribution ranging from northern New South Wales to central Victoria. They found 78.2 per cent similarity between populations, which they felt to be a high level of diversity, particularly as the populations were disjunct. However, caution was expressed as to the reliability of chloroplast analysis in *Eucalyptus nitens* as it was felt further analysis throughout the genus was needed in view of the high levels of diversity expressed.[23]

Godt and Hamrick used allozymes to study genetic diversity in *Elliottia racemosa* (Ericaceae), a rare shrub found at 50 locations, all within the state of Georgia, USA. They found low mean genetic diversity of 0.091 per cent, compared with mean genetic diversity of 0.249 per cent in 73 angiosperm tree species.[24] The authors attribute the lack of genetic diversity to the shrub's ability to reproduce via extensive root-sprouts, although they state that most diversity was within, rather between populations.[25] The authors report that little or no seedset had occurred. However, in view of the diversity within populations, it is possible that sexual reproduction had occurred in the past.

Angiolillo *et al.* looked at 90 individuals to study genetic diversity within and between populations of olive species (*Olea)* and relationships of species within the genus. They found that cultivars of *Olea europaea* clustered with an average similarity of 74 per cent; wild olives (believed to be a different form of *O. europaea*) clustered at 68 per cent and other species within the genus clustered at 48 per cent. These values gave a mean similarity of 63.33 per cent between species, both wild and cultivated. They felt that no significant differences existed between wild and cultivated olives, and thought that the lack of variation between the two was probably due to the complex process of olive domestication during the past 5,000 years, whereby propagation material has undergone 'an intense exchange' rather than a 'unidirectional flux from east to west' throughout the tree's range from Asia to the Mediterranean basin. However, the authors felt that the level of genetic diversity within the genus *Olea* is high, particularly in view of the duration and intensity of human influence.[26]

Yamanoto *et al.* studied genetic diversity within 24 chestnut varieties from five chestnut species, taken from individual trees in Japan, Korean Peninsula, China, France and USA. Percentage similarity between individuals ranged from 73 per cent to 94 per cent, which was felt by the authors to be a low level of diversity, probably due to the fact that most trees sampled were from cultivated rather than natural populations and therefore subject to selection pressure.[27]

Perera *et al.* studied genetic relationships between 42 coconut (*Cocus nucifera* L) accessions and found levels of genetic similarity in excess of 81 per cent. Three forms of coconut exist: tall (Typica); intermediate (Aurantiaca); and dwarf (Nana); most variation was detected within the Typica form.[28]

Drummond *et al.* studied genetic diversity in 31 surviving individuals of a rare New Zealand tree, *Metrosideros bartlettii,* and found 82 per cent diversity, which they considered to be high.[29]

European genetic studies on *P. nigra* L

Legionnet and Lefevre studied variation in 60 trees from Bulgaria, Romanian, Slovakia, Hungary, Belgium and Italy, together with 111 examples from throughout France. They found that average diversity was greater in the non-French samples (74.9 per cent similarity, as against 80.1 per cent for the French samples). The authors found that within-stand differentiation was 3.5 per cent

FIGURE 48.
(a) Winter silhouette of an ivy-clad black poplar at Cruckton in Shropshire.
MIKE COOPER
(b) Winter silhouette of a tree near Church Stretton, which sadly fell in the winter of 2002/2003.
DAVE PHILLIPS
These pictures highlight the great morphological variation within the species.

and between-stand differentiation was 1.7 per cent, lower than averages previously found for long-lived, woody, outcrossing, wind-pollinated species, which are 7.6 per cent and 9.9 per cent respectively.[30]

Legionnet *et al.* investigated sexual and asexual reproduction of *P. nigra*, using 163 trees in six natural stands in western France. Of 118 trees in one site, only four pairs of identical genotypes were observed. The authors found that most reproduction in adult stands was sexual rather than vegetative, whilst that in juvenile stands tended to be vegetative, probably caused by epicormic growth resulting from root damage, and concluded that sexual and asexual reproduction of black poplar play complementary roles. However, they did not analyse the level of genetic diversity within the stands, which would have been a useful comparison to other diversity studies of *P. nigra*, particularly where sexual reproduction is known to have taken place.[31]

Heinze developed a genetic marker from an American hybrid poplar (*P. deltoides* x *P. trichocarpa* Torr.) to detect a *P. deltoides*-specific allele in black poplar hybrids. He was able to detect this allele in natural stands of *P. nigra* and from this he established the level of hybrid introgression. He found that the allele was present in seeds collected from hybrid individuals, but 'surprisingly low levels' were detected in individuals from the black poplars stands, although hybrid plantations were within pollinating distance.[32] The absence of the allele in the black poplar stands suggests that previous concerns about hybrid introgression in black poplar may be unfounded, although it is possible that genetic pollution of black poplar in Britain has occurred as a result of cultivation by nurserymen in the past.

A study by Arens *et al.* found an average of 82.7 per cent similarity between 143 *P. nigra* individuals on the banks of the Dutch Rhine system. The subspecies in the study was unknown, but was likely to have been *P. nigra* subsp *betulifolia*, since the study was conducted in western Europe, where subsp *betulifolia* is found. Although the level of diversity found (82.7 per cent) was greater than that found within black poplar in the British Isles, it was nevertheless felt by the authors to be low.[33]

A study by van der Schoot *et al.* investigated genetic diversity within 23 trees from the EUFORGEN Core Collection of black poplar individuals from throughout Europe.[34] These trees were selected for morphological diversity observed within the species (vast morphological differences can be observed throughout the range (Figure 48), as it was felt that morphological selection would conserve maximum genetic diversity.[35] They found 71 per cent similarity and felt that the total genetic diversity within the species may be higher than previously found. The collection includes two trees from Britain (Huntingdon female and Cambridge male), and these were found to be the most genetically similar trees in the study, supporting findings made by Cottrell *et al.*[36] and Winfield *et al.* (see below).[37]

Hughes *et al.* studied the effect of differing water table depths and sediment types on male and female black poplars, using an experimental site on an alluvial island in the River Great Ouse in Cambridgeshire. They found that females tended to prefer wetter and more nutrient-rich sites than males, which is thought by the authors to be due to the fact that they have to invest greater effort in reproductive strategies than males. However, they found that, although females showed higher growth rates than males, it was not statistically significant, suggesting that there was considerable overlap in the requirements of the sexes.[38]

Results from a study conducted by a consortium of researchers from throughout Europe indicated that the most distinctive trees were identified in the Danube region (Austria), the Rhone region (France), Italy, the Rijn region (The Netherlands), and the Ebro region (Spain). In general, the diversity was largest in the material collected from the regions in southern Europe. However, as clonal duplication was only 26 per cent, this suggests that mainland Europe has a greater level of genetic diversity than Britain.[39]

Analysis of *P. nigra* L subsp *betulifolia* in Britain

A study by Cottrell *et al.* on 36 accessions from individuals held in a clone bank, taken from trees throughout England and Wales, found an average of 94 per cent similarity, with 17 distinct genotypes, implying that 50 per cent of the population may be genetically identical. However, they feel that, in view of the geographical range, 50 per cent may be an over-estimate, as localised populations throughout the distribution are more likely to be clonal. Of six female trees in the sample, only two genotypes were identified, indicating that 33 per cent of females are distinct genotypes. This level of diversity appears to be lower in the subspecies than that found at species level, as the same authors found 77 per cent similarity in a study of *P. nigra.*[40]

Winfield *et al.* reported on the Environment Agency study of 146 accessions of black poplar in the Upper Severn Area, covering Shropshire, Montgomeryshire, north Worcestershire and south-west Staffordshire. Most of the trees on the national record, held by the Biological Records Centre of the Institute of Terrestrial Ecology, were sampled to evaluate the level of diversity in an area that had suffered comparatively little perturbation. Results from this study indicated that little genetic diversity exists in the area studied, with individual trees on average 97 per cent similar. One tree was identical to an individual 200 km away and most populations were found to be clonal, indicating that the species in Britain has been maintained by cuttings.[41]

Studies into the genetic diversity of hardwood species indicate that levels of diversity vary greatly. This suggests that more studies are needed on a greater number of genera to enable useful comparisons to be made. The lack of comparative studies is particularly marked in the study of black poplar, in that very little is known about the amount of genetic diversity present in other British hardwood species, and it is therefore difficult to ascertain whether *Populus* is in fact genetically depauperate, or whether high similarity is a characteristic of black poplar.

My study successfully analysed 170 trees using three separate primers. The samples were taken from trees from throughout the range, including specimens from the Republic of Ireland and Holland. Average overall similarity was 88.4 per cent. No specific differences were found between male and female trees, and a tree grown from seed was identical to other trees. The tree from Holland was identical to trees from Suffolk, Caernarvonshire, Leicestershire and Lancashire. Despite this, the level of diversity highlighted in this study is greater than that found by Cottrell *et al.* and Winfield *et al.* who found levels of 94 per cent and 97 per cent similarity respectively, but less than that suggested in the study by Arens *et al.*, who found 82.7 per cent similarity in trees from the Dutch Rhine river system.[42]

Comparisons with the studies of genetic diversity within the *Populus* genus indicate that greater levels of genetic diversity exist in other *Populus* species. *P. tremuloides* and *P. grandidentata* are approximately 68 per cent and 72 per cent similar; other studies on *P. tremuloides* have yielded variable results, ranging from 23.5 per cent to 42 per cent diversity.

Comparisons with studies on woody species suggest the same. The levels of genetic diversity in the species studied were: *Eucalyptus nitens*, 78.2 per cent similarity; *Grevillea scapigera*, 75 per cent; *Camellia sinensis*, 69.5 per cent; *Cocus nucifera* L, average 81 per cent; *Castanea* sp., average 83.5 per cent; *Olea* sp., average 63.33 per cent; *Moringa oleifera*, average 70.51 per cent. This indicates that average genetic diversity is lower in black poplar than other woody species – something that is now a great cause for concern, in view of the recent appearance of the pathogen *Venturia populina*.

CHAPTER SIX

Conservation Strategies

Research and conservation groups in Britain and Europe

Largely as a result of Edgar Milne-Redhead's enthusiasm and love for black poplar, various working groups concerned with conservation of black poplar have evolved since the early 1990s, both in Britain and in mainland Europe. These groups operate at differing levels and angles of interest, with some groups studying genetic diversity on an international scale and others surveying trees at county level. Even individual people in their respective local parishes contribute towards the conservation effort.

In 1993, a group of individuals interested in conservation of black poplar met in London and formed the Black Poplar Working Group. This meeting resulted in the production of *The Native Black Poplar in Britain: An Action Plan for its Conservation*, written in 1994 by Jonathan Spencer of English Nature. The Action Plan was the first document produced by a statutory nature conservation body to address the status of black poplar in Britain, and to propose action for the recording of trees, necessary for genetic study and planting programmes. However, since its publication, no updated document has been produced, and as our knowledge of black poplar ecology and genetic diversity has greatly increased in the interim period, it is now important to disseminate this information into a national action plan, in order to bring together the efforts of groups working in the field of black poplar conservation and to ensure the tree's continued survival.

In 1994, the European Forest Genetic Resources Programme (EUFORGEN) network was founded to introduce a co-ordinated policy for gene conservation in woody species. The group identified four pilot species: *Picea abies*; *P. nigra*; *Quercus suber*; and Rosaceae (the noble hardwoods). The network is operative under the aegis of the International Board for Plant Genetic Resources and the Forest Department of the Food and Agriculture Organisation. The group meets annually to report upon national strategies for conservation of the pilot species. A sub-group known as Europop was set up by members of the EUFORGEN *P. nigra* Network to study the genetic diversity of trees along Europe's river systems. The group consists of workers from Austria, Belgium, Britain, France, Germany, Holland, Italy and Spain and is funded by Commission of the European Communities, Agriculture and Fisheries (FAIR) specific research and technical development (RTD) programme, PL97–3386.

The project is known as 'Genetic diversity in river populations of European Black Poplar for evaluation of biodiversity, conservation strategies, nature development and genetic improvement'.[1]

Between 1995 and 1999 a small group of British researchers, known unofficially as the National Black Poplar Working Group, met annually to discuss progress in different aspects of academic research into black poplar conservation. Unfortunately, due to the divergent activities of some members of the group in recent years, its existence is unlikely to continue. However, largely as a result of the large black poplar population in the Vale of Aylesbury, a local group, supported by the Aylesbury Vale Countryside Service, was formed in 1996. In view of interest in the species nationally, this group rapidly grew to become the UK Black Poplar Conservation Group in 2000 and now meets biennially to report upon all levels of conservation activity and research into black poplar.

In 2000, the FLOBAR project was implemented: this was a three-year multidisciplinary project, funded by the EU 'Energy, Environment and Sustainable Development' Programme of the Fifth Framework Programme, and consisted of a group of academics from the USA and Europe researching various aspects of floodplain forest ecology, geomorphology and hydrology.[2] Floodplain forests are spatially complex mosaics of small-scale patches of different forest types, often interspersed with wetland and grassland ecosystems. They are most extensive when associated with meandering or braided floodplain areas. The group meets annually to discuss issues pertaining to floodplain forest management, a topic clearly pertinent to black poplar conservation.

Local and regional projects also exist in Britain. In Darlington, Co. Durham, a conservation project was started in 2000 to conserve existing black poplars, and to plant around 500 trees in the borough by 2005. A local folk singer, Vin Garbutt, has produced a CD to publicise and promote the project and the plight of the species; a poster, postcard and leaflet have also been produced.[3] A joint experimental project between Severn Trent Water (STW) and the National Forest Company (NFC), in association with Middlemarch Environmental, has also recently begun, investigating the recreation of floodplain forest and wet woodland throughout the National Forest in the Midlands.[4]

The necessity for conservation of black poplar in Britain

Tabbush suggests three pressing reasons for the conservation of the black poplar: such action is compatible with the biodiversity agreement signed by Britain in 1992 at the Rio Summit, where Britain's representatives agreed to protect national biodiversity; the species has commercial importance as one parent of the hybrid *P. euramericana*, and is both easy to propagate and resistant to the pathogens *Xanthamonas populi* and *Marssonina brunnea*; and a lack of natural regeneration, coupled with the fact that the population is even-aged, means that the species could become extinct within 20–30 years.[5]

Other reasons may be added to the list given above. The species supports a range of invertebrates with specific habitat requirements that are not found on other species. Additionally, with so much research currently being undertaken into floodplain forest management, it is important to conserve the tree, which is generally considered to be an integral element of such habitats, for use in future restoration schemes. The genus *Populus* is becoming widely used as a model for various genetic studies,[6] rather as *Arabidopsis* is the genetic model for the plant world. In addition to these, there are other, perhaps less scientific, reasons why black poplar should be the subject of a conservation programme. The tree's links with literature and folklore, coupled with its rarity, have endowed it with an aura of mystery, which adds to the appeal of conservation strategies. It can also be argued that the tree should be conserved as it is a significant landscape feature; despite Gilbert-Carter's opinion that groves of the tree 'present a grotesque appearance',[7] they are a truly dramatic sight. Timber from black poplar plantations can be utilised in the restoration of buildings where original poplar timbers were used. Finally, it should be not forgotten that the tree holds an important place in public sympathies.[8] It was evident during fieldwork for this study that landowners were, in the main, fond of their tree or trees and frequently knew a great deal about the species and the history of their specimens.[9]

Suggestions for conservation strategies

The popularity of black poplar has resulted in a number of ad hoc planting schemes throughout Britain, many of which are commendable, others perhaps less so. For example, some 500 black poplars have been planted along a seven kilometre stretch of village bypass in Shropshire. Because of the close proximity in which the trees have been planted, they will not achieve the familiar form of black poplar, and will doubtless cause problems for the highway authorities in years to come, as they characteristically shed their limbs. In contrast, an excellent scheme is being undertaken in Newcastle upon Tyne, where cuttings being taken from three lovely old trees growing in the churchyard of All Saints church (Figure 49) are destined for planting in a nearby Victorian park, which is being restored by Southern Green Landscape Architects.[10] This is both historically and ecologically appropriate, given the park's proximity to the River Tyne, and provided the trees are managed in a suitable manner (that is, shredded or pollarded), the scheme should not cause problems in the future.

The results of my study,[11] and previous studies on British black poplar,[12] indicate that there are no biological reasons why one individual tree should be favoured over another in any planting or conservation strategy. However, the historical aspect of the study has highlighted the fact that, for historical and cultural reasons, it is desirable to use local trees when planning clone banks or planting programmes. It is also desirable to maintain the morphological variation between trees in eastern, western and northern areas, despite the fact that the reasons for these variations are unclear.

Conservation Strategies

A British ex situ conservation strategy already exists, in the form of a collection of black poplars from throughout the country that is held in a national clone bank in Norfolk. This clone bank should now perhaps be extended to include a tree from each clonal grouping identified by the author's study, together with trees of each sex, which display the differing leaf morphology characteristics.

It is desirable to utilise *in situ* methods to ensure the continued survival of black poplar in its natural habitat. Any planting programme should make provision for long-term planting; the population is currently even-aged, with many trees currently reaching the end of their natural lifespan. Large numbers of trees are being planted at present, and in the event of black poplar remaining a fashionable topic for only a few years, there is the danger that this approach would merely postpone the problem and would leave botanists of the future desperately trying to save the species, rather as we are doing today.

Planting and management guidelines

I am very grateful to Marianne Jones of the Environment Agency for providing me with her draft guidelines on the protection, planting and management of trees, which I have adapted in the following paragraphs.

Protection of existing trees and in situ conservation

It is essential to conserve existing trees. Black poplar, as with any other mature tree, should be protected from changes in soil or water table levels. Compaction of the soil around the tree must be prevented, as must fires below the canopy. Severe damage can be caused to trees by grazing animals and ploughing; ideally trees should be fenced off at a generous distance and, in a related point, it is worth considering that the roots of a poplar will spread to a radius of about 1.5 times its height. Surgery may be appropriate for old, damaged trees, if it may prolong the life of the tree, but any work of this kind should be carried out with the utmost caution (see below).

FIGURE 49. Black poplars in the churchyard of All Saints' church in Newcastle-on-Tyne (together with one hybrid). It is possible that they are relicts of a natural population that grew alongside the River Tyne. However, they may have resulted from the supply of the incorrect species by nurseries.
MIKE COOPER

Pollards

Many black poplars have been pollarded in the past, especially in the Vale of Aylesbury, East Anglia, Derbyshire, Herefordshire, Worcestershire and Gloucestershire. This is a traditional form of management and it is very important that trees are re-pollarded at regular intervals. When carried out carefully, this practice can extend the life of the tree, and it is believed that many black poplar pollards in Britain live to a greater age than those left to grow naturally (Figure 50).[13] In addition, use of the practice ensures the continuation of a distinctive landscape feature.

When re-pollarding it is important to protect the area known as the branch collar (a ring of bark where the branch joins the trunk). It is sometimes worth considering cutting the tree in two or more stages, several years apart, particularly where a tree has not been trimmed for many years. At the first stage the upper branches are removed; after a period of one to five years the second cut can bring the crown down to a lower level, retaining some of the new growth produced as a result of the first cut. The ideal times for re-pollarding are spring and autumn. January to March is the optimal time for the benefit of the tree, and minimises disturbance to associated wildlife. Work should not be carried out during or immediately after a period of drought or severe cold, as this is believed to render the tree more vulnerable to various fungal infections that attack the bark or leaves. There is some suggestion that the drier conditions in the east of the country may make re-pollarding more difficult and can cause death of the tree.[14]

Caution should be exercised when re-pollarding; over-vigorous cutting can lead to the death of the tree. When carrying out any type of surgery to a tree that has suffered years of neglect, it is desirable to leave two or three branches, or to conduct the work over two or three years. Some groups in Aylesbury have found that a significant number of trees have died after re-pollarding (see Chapter Three) and suggest that re-pollarding is not always the best option for the tree. However, it should be borne in mind that further research is necessary on this topic. Nevertheless, it is important that the age and condition of the tree are considered prior to any major surgery, and a reputable tree surgeon will be able to advise. Older trees and those that have not been pollarded for many years may struggle to recover from the work.[15] In the case of such trees, where the work is absolutely necessary, it is recommended that cuttings are taken for replanting and that the style of the work is carefully considered. If there are a number of trees on site in the same condition it is important to stagger the work, thereby testing the methods employed. It is also vital to take photographs and make records of the work undertaken.

Carrying out tree surgery is an extremely dangerous occupation and should always be carried out be a fully qualified certificated operator, wearing full protective clothing. In most cases it is necessary to have certificates for using a chainsaw at height, and for tree climbing; these should be checked by whoever is responsible for site safety.

New pollards can be created when the girth of a young sapling reaches about 150–200 mm. The tree is cut, usually between 2–4 m from the ground, to cause it to bush out. It is important to gain a management commitment when creating new pollards since re-pollarding is essential and should be carried out on a 10–15 year cycle. During the establishment period this could be reduced to every 3–5 years.

Traditional methods of propagation

Black poplar can be propagated via seed or cuttings, although in practice the latter route has been most used. Evelyn recommended the planting of truncheons, seven or eight feet long, in the ground.[16] This mode of propagation was also recommended by Cook, who suggested that planting in wet ground, using 'truncheons around 2–8 ft long', was a productive method.[17] This is an approach that has been successfully used in recent years in the Vale of

Aylesbury, where cuttings 1.5 m long have grown to 3 m within two to three years.[18] Loudon, cited in Elwes and Henry, also describes how the tree grows easily from cuttings,[19] but does not elaborate on suitable cutting sizes. Today, nurserymen recommend taking cuttings approximately 25 cm long in February or March and placing them in damp ground, from which a 50 per cent success rate can be expected. Natural vegetative reproduction frequently occurs if a fallen tree or branch is left undisturbed on damp ground, where it can take root and continue to grow.[20] Similarly, broken branches from riverside trees can be washed downstream and embedded into riverbanks, eventually forming new trees.

When planning a planting scheme, careful consideration should also be given to the ratio between male and female trees. Female trees are popular because of their rarity but it is important to remember the problems which can be caused by the copious amounts of fluffy seeds that are produced.

Selecting a tree for propagation

Very often, older trees will lack the suitable young growth required for cuttings, but they can often form vigorous epicormic shoots from their trunks that are suitable for propagation material. In addition, newly cut pollards are an excellent source of material of varying sizes.

Poplar will grow from hardwood or softwood cuttings; the latter require more elaborate horticultural technology. Hardwood cuttings are taken in the autumn and winter when the tree is largely dormant and the current year's wood has ripened, but when root growth still takes place. Softwood cuttings are best taken between the end of July and end of August. It is possible to continue into October, but success rates are poor. Since very good results can be obtained from hardwood cuttings, it is likely that this will be the most common method chosen. Softwood cuttings may be considered in an emergency situation if a tree collapses or has to be felled during the summer months. Whilst hardwood cuttings can be taken any time over the dormant months, cuttings taken before Christmas usually start to root quickly and these may then be broken by frost heave in the soil during the latter part of the winter. Many have reported that cuttings taken in February and March have been extremely successful.

Cuttings should be taken from new growth made in the previous summer. They should be 15–20 cm long with at least half their length below ground. The cuttings can be rooted straight into the open ground. It is also possible to grow them in containers, in a mixture of sand and soil, which should be kept damp; once rooted, they can then be planted in open ground. Weed control is very important over the first year and can be achieved by the use of black plastic or felt mulch. Rooted cuttings can usually be planted out after their first year. They should be protected from damage by rabbits or other grazing animals and surrounding weed growth should be controlled for the first few years. In order to relieve pressure on native trees, save time in collecting material and produce vigorous cutting material, the establishment of stool beds is recommended. Cuttings must be accurately labelled during their life in the nursery.

To establish new trees by using 'truncheons' (large cuttings), the cuttings must be planted directly on site. Sections of young branch about 5–10 cm in diameter and 1.5 m long can be used. Use a bar to make a hole and bury the cutting to approximately one third of its length. The surrounding soil should be firmed and the new tree protected in the usual way.

Propagation using tissue culture

A more modern method of plant propagation is that of tissue culture (*in vitro* culture), where plants are regenerated from explants (small cuttings) of leaves and other plant organs. This is a useful method of propagation for the conservation of endangered species if the use of more traditional methods would be detrimental to a species: for example, where very low numbers of individuals exist. Propagation can be from either sterile or non-sterile mother plants; however, propagation from non-sterile plants is quicker and simpler. The explant (approximately 2 cm^2 of plant tissue) is placed in a petri dish containing agar (a gel made from seaweed), the dish is sealed with plastic film and incubated at 25° Celcius with continuous white fluorescent light for up to ten weeks, depending upon the development of the explant. Once adventitious buds and roots have developed, the explants can be transferred to covered, ventilated seed trays containing compost for around ten weeks before transferring to larger pots in a greenhouse.[21]

The tissue culture method of propagation has been applied to *P. alba* and *P. canescens* species, with a greater level of success than with the conventional method of growing cuttings in a greenhouse. However, it is perhaps unnecessary to employ tissue culture propagation methods to black poplar, as it readily regenerates by vegetative means.

Nursery supplies and seeds

Whilst some nurseries are carefully sourcing and propagating native black poplar, others are not, and it is essential that genuine stock are supplied. Native black poplar will hybridise with many other poplars that flower at the same time and, as the estimated radius for pollen travel is about 16 km, it is possible that many seeds are genetically polluted;[22] therefore, propagation from seed is not recommended.

Suitable planting sites

There are several practical guidelines that need to be taken into consideration when choosing a site to plant black poplars. When looking for planting sites in your area it is important to study the local distributions of the species which exist (if any) and emulate these where possible. Thought should also be given to the creation of new pollards. This choice may be made in order to ensure the continuation of a valuable landscape feature, or from a practical point of view, to save space.

FIGURE 50.
Newly-pollarded black poplar on the traffic island at Powick.
DAVE PHILLIPS

There is a growing interest amongst conservation bodies in the restoration of floodplain forest, and demonstration sites are being developed in Milton Keynes and mid Wales. In these conditions, black poplar grow close together and tall, giving way to oak and elm on drier land. Sadly, however, no matter how accurately we try to reproduce these conditions, hybridisation will always prevent complete re-establishment.

New trees must be planted well away from any structures and underground services. As mentioned earlier, it is estimated that the root systems of black poplar affect the ground for a distance with a radius that is at least one and a half times the height of the tree. Care should also be taken when planting trees by roadsides, public footpaths and amenity areas, as the tree can become brittle when it is aged around 75–100 years, and is therefore dangerous.

The ability of any species of poplar to dry out the ground needs to be considered carefully when introducing new black poplars to an area of existing wetland habitat or adjacent to an area of archaeological importance. It is important to ensure that damage is not inflicted upon existing features. Likewise, the effects of shade and leaf fall on the existing habitat need to be considered. Planting sites will ideally be in full light with good moisture supply and a lowland climate. Black poplar is not a shade-tolerant tree and if not given plenty of light will be prevented from developing its characteristic silhouette; for this reason also, trees should be planted at least 20 m apart.[23]

Black poplars are normally found on alluvial soils although they have also been found on the lower slopes of upland areas, particularly along the Welsh border, and provided there is an adequate water supply, such as an underground spring, or high rainfall, combined with water-retentive soil, altitude should not pose a threat. Water quality in adjacent watercourses does not seem to be a critical factor and black poplars may benefit from nutrient enrichment. Black poplar does not thrive in acid soil.

Planting numbers and strategy

Since the national population is of an even age that is largely mature, it is essential that a long-term planting strategy be implemented over a 50–100 year period. This is, of course, impossible for one person to achieve but it is hoped that, using continued promotion and education, an ongoing programme can be ensured.

There is controversy regarding the numbers of young trees that should be planted. However, to keep current population figures stable it is necessary to plant between 7–10 trees to ensure one individual tree reaches maturity. Views regarding planting numbers vary considerably, and are often personal and hard to define. The large size of black poplar individuals at maturity means that the species is best planted singly or in small groups. Large-scale use in landscaping schemes is probably inappropriate in most situations, other than in the creation of floodplain forest. Many maintain that, since the species is rare, it is important not to plant it too widely, and it certainly thrives best as a solitary tree. Rackham suggests that small-leaved lime is being devalued by becoming commonplace,[24] and it can be argued that the same sentiment applies to black poplar, in that its appeal lies in its rarity; in a similar manner, Marren discusses the delight of stumbling across rare plants in the countryside.[25]

Ex situ conservation

A number of *populeta* have been established by the Forestry Commission, which comprises of 36 clones of selected black poplar individuals from throughout England and Wales; these have been grown to maintain a collection of genetic material. However, recent genetic analysis means that a review of the content of these collections should now be carried out. In addition to the national collection, several counties, including Cheshire and Suffolk, have set up clone banks of local material, which are sources of material for anyone wishing to obtain cuttings.[26]

I cannot emphasise strongly enough the urgent need for cuttings to be taken from trees that are currently free of *Venturia populina*, in order that we have accessible clone banks of what are, hopefully, disease resistant clones. It is to be hoped that local councils and wildlife trusts will take a lead in this direction.

Future research and conservation needs

The scope for further research is vast. Analysis of chloroplast and mitochondrial DNA may reveal differences between the sexes of black poplar, and may also show greater levels of genetic diversity to support the morphological variation that is present. In addition, new methods of genetic analysis are constantly being developed, and this, coupled with evolving sequence information, will undoubtedly further our knowledge regarding both genetic diversity and disease resistance. As far as the conservation of the species is concerned, a recording system that makes provision for ecologically and historically important trees and approximate age of trees should be implemented and the full recording of currently unlisted trees in Vale of Aylesbury, Manchester and other counties should be conducted, together with sexing of those trees whose gender is uncertain. Further work in the Republic of Ireland is likely to locate more trees, as Desmond Hobson's survey took place by car and thus only recorded roadside trees. Research into the loss of trees following pollarding, which has occurred throughout the range, is of immediate significance. Perhaps most importantly, urgent research is needed into the disease *V. populina*, and a strategy must be developed to minimise its impact, since as things stand it is likely to devastate the national population; little is known about the disease, as it has only been observed in very recent years.

The future for the tree

Despite the various conservation and planting projects that are being undertaken throughout Britain, and the species' ability to regenerate in a vegetative manner, the future for black poplar appears to be somewhat precarious at present. Planting programmes will need to be carefully planned in order to minimise the destruction caused by *V. populina*, which appears to pose a severe threat to the genetically depauperate population, which does not seem to be resistant to this disease; and any large population should be carefully monitored for signs of disease. However, it is possible that isolated trees may be at less of a risk. It is very difficult to accurately describe or even imagine how the loss of the population would affect those landscapes where the tree is abundant; it would be very sad indeed to lose this magnificent tree from our landscape.

Notes to the Chapters

Notes to Chapter One: Cultural and Botanical Features of the Black Poplar

1. D. E. Allen (1976) *The Naturalist in Britain*, Penguin, Harmondsworth.
2. K. Thomas (1983) *Man and the Natural World*, Allen Lane, London.
3. D. Evans (1992) *A History of Nature Conservation in Britain*, Routledge, London.
4. K. Thomas, *Man and the Natural World*.
5. D. Evans, *A History of Nature Conservation in Britain*.
6. D. Evans, *A History of Nature Conservation in Britain*.
7. R. Hayman (2003) *Trees: Woodlands and Western Civilization*, Hambledon and London, London.
8. S. Cohen (1999) 'Promoting Eden: Tree planting as the environmental panacea', *Ecumene* **6**, 4, 424–446.
9. R. Hayman, *Trees: Woodlands and Western Civilization*.
10. S. Schama (1995) *Landscape and Memory*, Harper Collins, London.
11. K. Thomas, *Man and the Natural World*.
12. S. Cohen, 'Promoting Eden: Tree planting as the environmental panacea'.
13. C. D. Klemm and C. Shine (1993) *Biodiversity Conservation and the Law*, IUCN, Gland, Switzerland and Cambridge, UK.
14. C. Watkins (1983) 'The public control of woodland management', *The Town Planning Review* **54**, 4, 437–464.
15. C. Booker (21 January 1999) 'How a decaying old tree and officious bureaucracy cost me thousands – and nearly branded me a criminal', *Daily Mail*.
16. O. Rackham (1986) *The History of the Countryside*, Weidenfield & Nicholson, London.
17. J. White (1993) *Black Poplar: the most endangered native timber tree in Britain*, Forestry Authority.
18. D. Craddock (1999) *Genetic variation in the black poplar (Populus nigra L. subsp betulifolia (Pursh) W. Wettst). Molecular variation female/male black poplar using chloroplast and mitochondrial specific primers*, Undergraduate dissertation in the School of Biological Sciences, The University of Nottingham, Nottingham.
19. E. Milne-Redhead (1985) 'In pursuit of the poplar', *Natural World* **10**, 26–28.
20. D. D. Hobson (1991) *The black poplar in Ireland: its distribution and origin*, St John's College, The University of Oxford, Oxford.
21. E. Milne-Redhead, 'In pursuit of the poplar'.
22. E. Milne-Redhead, 'In pursuit of the poplar'; D. D. Hobson, pers. comm.
23. E. Milne-Redhead, 'In pursuit of the poplar'
24. E. Milne-Redhead, 'In pursuit of the poplar'.
25. G. F. Peterken and F. M. R. Hughes (1995) 'Restoration of floodplain forests in Britain', *Forestry* **68**, 3, 187–202; P. Tabbush (1995) 'Native poplars and the restoration of floodplain forests', *Quarterly Journal of Forestry* **90**, 128–134.
26. O. Rackham (1990) *Trees and Woodland in the British Landscape*, Dent, London.; J. E. J. White (1993) *Genetic Pollution of British Native Black Poplar, Populus nigra subsp betulifolia (Pursh) W. Wettst*, Symposium on Black Poplar, London, unpublished.
27. J. E. J. White, *Genetic Pollution of British Native Black Poplar*.
28. H. Ellenberg (1988) *Vegetation Ecology of Central Europe*, Cambridge University Press, Cambridge.
29. G. F. Peterken and F. M. R. Hughes, 'Restoration of floodplain forests in Britain'.
30. N. Barsoum, pers. comm.
31. A. G. Tansley (1949) *Britain's Green Mantle*, George Allen & Unwin Ltd, London.
32. G. F. Peterken (1996) *Natural Woodland*, Cambridge University Press, Cambridge.
33. W. J. Bean (1976; 8th ed.) *Trees and Shrubs Hardy in the British Isles*, John Murray, London.
34. I. V. Splunder, H. Coops, L. A. C. J. Voesenek and C. W. P. M. Blom (1996) 'Morphological responses of seedlings of four species of Salicaceae to drought', *Canadian Journal of Botany* **74**, 1988–1995.
35. J. Evelyn (1664) *Sylva: or a discourse on forest trees*, J. Martyn & J. Allesby, London.

36. M. Cook (1724) *Manners of Raising and Ordering Fruit Trees*, Elizabeth Bell, London.
37. H. Gilbert-Carter (1932) *Our Catkin-Bearing Plants: An Introduction*, Oxford University Press, London.
38. R. D. Meikle (1984) *Willows and Poplars of Great Britain and Ireland*, BSBI Handbook No. 4, Botanical Society of the British Isles, London.
39. L. Zsuffa (1974) 'The genetics of Populus nigra L.' *Annales Forestales Anali Za Sumarstvo* **6**, 2, 29–49.
40. W. N. Stewart (1983) *Paleobotany and the evolution of plants*, Cambridge University Press, Cambridge.
41. J. R. Matthews (1955) *Origin and Distribution of the British Flora*, Hutchinson's University Library, London.
42. H. Godwin (1975; 2nd ed.) *The History of the British Flora*, Cambridge University Press, Cambridge.
43. H. J. Elwes and A. Henry (1913) *The Trees of Great Britain and Ireland*, Edinburgh.
44. W. B. R. Laidlaw (1960) *Guide to British Hardwoods*, Leonard Hill (Books) Ltd, London.
45. H. Gilbert-Carter (1936) *British Trees and Shrubs*, Clarendon Press, Oxford.
46. J. White, pers. comm.
47. W. J. Bean, *Trees and Shrubs Hardy in the British Isles.*
48. J. White, *Black Poplar: the most endangered native timber tree in Britain.*
49. R. D. Meikle, pers. comm.
50. A. Henry (1914) 'The Black Poplars', *The Gardeners' Chronicle* **56**, 1–2, 66–67; G. S. Cansdale (1938) *The Black Poplars, and their Hybrids Cultivated in Britain*, Oxford University Press, Oxford.
51. H. Gilbert-Carter, *British Trees and Shrubs.*
52. D. D. Hobson, pers. comm.
53. E. Step (1940) *Wayside and Woodland Trees*, Frederick Warne & Co. Ltd, London; T. R. Peace (1952) *Poplars*, Forestry Commission Bulletin No. 19, HMSO, London.
54. G. S. Cansdale, *The Black Poplars, and their Hybrids Cultivated in Britain.*
55. J. M. Paterson (1996) *Tree Wisdom*, Thorsons, London.
56. H. J. Elwes and A. Henry, *The Trees of Great Britain and Ireland*; E. Step, *Wayside and Woodland Trees*; A. Mitchell and J. Wilkinson (1988; 2nd ed.) *Trees of Britain and Northern Europe*, Collins, London.
57. H. J. Elwes and A. Henry, *The Trees of Great Britain and Ireland.*
58. A. Henry, 'The Black Poplars'; T. R. Peace, *Poplars.*
59. A. Henry, 'The Black Poplars'.
60. J. Jobling (1990) *Poplars for Wood Production and Amenity*, Forestry Commission Bulletin No. 92, HMSO, London.
61. J. E. J. White, *Genetic Pollution of British Native Black Poplar.*
62. J. Evelyn, *Sylva.*
63. O. Rackham, *The History of the Countryside.*
64. O. Rackham, *The History of the Countryside.*
65. Anon. (1927) *Official Guide to the Metropolitan Borough of Poplar*, ed. A.o.t. P. B. Council, J. Burrow & Co. Ltd, Cheltenham.
66. Anon. (1933) 'Poplar in the past', in *The Copartnership Herald.*
67. M. Cook, *Manners of Raising and Ordering Fruit Trees.*
68. G. Grigson (1958) *An Englishman's Flora*, Helicon Publishing Ltd, Oxford.
69. E. Gutch and M. Peacock (1908) *Examples of printed folk-lore concerning Lincolnshire*, Folk Lore Society, London.
70. H. L. Edlin (1985) *Broadleaves*, Forestry Commission Booklet No. 20, HMSO, London.
71. C. A. Stace (1991) *New Flora of the British Isles*, Cambridge University Press, Cambridge; J. White (1993) *Black Poplar: the most endangered native timber tree in Britain.*
72. B. Huntley and H. J. B. Birks (1983) *An atlas of past and present pollen maps for Europe: 0–13,000 years ago*, Cambridge University Press, Cambridge.
73. J. E. J. White, *Genetic Pollution of British Native Black Poplar.*
74. H. Godwin, *The History of the British Flora.*
75. W. B. Turrill (1962) *British Plant Life*, Collins, London.
76. W. Pennington (1970) 'Vegetation history in north-west England' in *Studies in the vegetational history of the British Isles*, eds D. Walker and R. G. West, Cambridge University Press, Cambridge.
77. A. R. Clapham, T. G. Tutin and E. F. Warburg (1962) *Flora of the British Isles*, Cambridge University Press, Cambridge.
78. A. R. Clapham, T. G. Tutin and E. F. Warburg, *Flora of the British Isles.*
79. J. White, *Black Poplar: the most endangered native timber tree in Britain.*
80. P. Ennis, pers. comm.
81. J. White, *Black Poplar: the most endangered native timber tree in Britain*; P. Roe (1994) 'A cutting edge for the poplar hunt', *Daily Telegraph.*
82. E. Milne-Redhead (1990) 'The BSBI Black Poplar survey', *Watsonia* **18**, 1–5.
83. J. White, *Black Poplar: the most endangered native timber tree in Britain.*
84. D. D. Hobson, pers. comm.
85. J. Croft, pers. comm.
86. P. Roe, 'A cutting edge for the poplar hunt'.
87. E. Rogers (1995) 'The native black poplar (Populus nigra var. betulifolia (Pursh) Torr)', *Quarterly Journal of Forestry* **89**, 33–37.

88. G. C. Druce (1927) *The Flora of Oxfordshire*, Clarendon Press, Oxford.
89. C. E. J. Kennedy and T. R. E. Southwood (1984) 'The number of species of insects associated with British trees: A re-analysis', *Journal of Animal Ecology* **53**, 455–478.
90. T. James, pers. comm.
91. P. Tabbush (1995) 'Native poplars and the restoration of floodplain forests'.
92. S. M. Haslam (1991) *The Historic River*, Cobden of Cambridge, Cambridge.
93. J. Purseglove (1988) *Taming the Flood*, Oxford University Press, Oxford; S. M. Haslam, *The Historic River*.
94. G. F. Peterken and F. M. R. Hughes, 'Restoration of floodplain forests in Britain'.
95. J. Purseglove, *Taming the Flood*.
96. J. H. Braatne, S. B. Rood and P. E. Heilman (1996) 'Life history, ecology, and conservation of riparian cottonwoods in North America' in *Biology of Populus*, eds R. F. Stettler, H. D. Bradshaw Jr., P. E. Heilman and T. M. Hinckley, NRC Research Press, Ottawa.
97. W. B. Turrill, *British Plant Life*.
98. I. V. Splunder *et al.*, 'Morphological responses of seedlings of four species of Salicaceae to drought'.
99. I. V. Splunder *et al.*, 'Morphological responses of seedlings of four species of Salicaceae to drought'.
100. W. J. Bean, *Trees and Shrubs Hardy in the British Isles*.
101. J. White, pers. comm.
102. S. Bisoffi, pers. comm.
103. A. Legionnet, P. Faivre-Rampant, M. Villar and F. Lefevre (1997) 'Sexual and asexual reproduction in natural stands of Populus nigra', *Botanica Acta* **110**, 3, 257–263.
104. E. Rogers, pers. comm.
105. S. C. Holland (1992) *The Black Poplar in Gloucestershire*, FWAG, Gloucester.
106. W. Watson, pers. comm.
107. C. Alstrom-Rapaport, M. Laxcoux, Y. C. Wang, G. Roberts and G. A. Tuskan (1998) 'Identification of RAPD Marker Linked to Sex Determination in the Basket Willow (Salix viminalis L)', *Journal of Heredity* **89**, 44–49.
108. M. O. Winfield and F. M. R. Hughes (2002) 'Variation in Populus nigra clones: Implications for river restoration projects in the United Kingdom', *Wetlands* **22**, 1, 33–48.
109. J. C. Loudon (1854) *Arboretum et Fruticetum*.
110. H. J. Elwes and A. Henry, *The Trees of Great Britain and Ireland*.
111. J. Jobling, *Poplars for Wood Production and Amenity*.
112. J. White, pers. comm.
113. J. Evelyn, *Sylva*.
114. J. White, pers. comm.
115. G. Halliday (1997) *A Flora of Cumbria*, University of Lancaster, Centre for North West Regional Studies, Lancaster.
116. J. White, pers. comm.
117. E. Milne-Redhead, 'The BSBI Black Poplar survey'; S. Falk, pers. comm.
118. H. Beismann, J. H. A. Barker, A. Karp and T. Speck (1997) 'AFLP analysis sheds light on distribution of two Salix species and their hybrid along a natural gradient', *Molecular Ecology* **6**, 989–993.

Notes to Chapter Two: The Black Poplar in History

1. O. Rackham (1986) *The History of the Countryside*, Weidenfield & Nicholson, London.
2. O. Rackham, *The History of the Countryside*.
3. W. Linnard (1982) *Welsh Woods and Forests: History and Utilisation*, National Museum of Wales, Cardiff.
4. J. Evelyn (1664) *Sylva: or a discourse on forest trees*, J. Martyn & J. Allesby, London.
5. W. Linnard, *Welsh Woods and Forests: History and Utilisation.*
6. C. Threlkeld (1727) *Synopsis Stirpium Hibernicarum*, F. Davys, R. Norris & J. Worrall, Dublin.
7. H. L. Edlin (1945) *British Woodland Trees*, B. T. Batsford Ltd, London.
8. H. L. Edlin (1956) *Trees, Woods and Man*, Collins, London.
9. H. L. Edlin (1985) *Broadleaves*, HMSO, London.
10. E. Step (1940) *Wayside and Woodland Trees*, Frederick Warne & Co. Ltd, London.
11. P. Edwards (1962) *Trees and the English Landscape*, G. Bell & Sons, London.
12. F. H. Perring and S. M. Walters (1962) *Atlas to the British Flora*, T. Nelson, London.
13. E. Milne-Redhead (1990) 'The BSBI Black Poplar survey', *Watsonia* **18**, 1–5.
14. A. Mitchell and J. Wilkinson (1988) *Trees of Britain and Northern Europe*, Collins, London.
15. O. Rackham (1995) *Trees and Woodland in the British Landscape*, Weidenfield & Nicolson, London.
16. M. Snookes (1986) *Castlemorton Common: A handbook for locals and visitors*, Castlemorton Common Association.
17. O. Rackham, *The History of the Countryside*.
18. O. Rackham, *Trees and Woodland in the British Landscape*.
19. O. Rackham, *The History of the Countryside*.

20. H. L. Edlin (1969) *What wood is that?*, Thames & Hudson Ltd, Hertford.
21. P. J. Selby (1842) *A History of British Forest Trees Indigenous and Introduced*, John Van Voorst, London.
22. C. Watkins, S. Holland and S. Thompson (1997) *A survey of black poplars (Populus nigra L.) in Herefordshire*, The University of Nottingham, Nottingham.
23. W. Jones, pers. comm.
24. R. Mabey (1996) *Flora Britannica*, Sinclair-Stevenson, London.
25. K. Trimmer (1866) *Flora of Norfolk*, Norwich, London; J. Evelyn, *Sylva*.
26. R. Harris (1974) 'Poplar crucks in Worcestershire and Herefordshire', *Vernacular Architecture* 5, 25; J. Evelyn, *Sylva*; K. Trimmer, *Flora of Norfolk*; E. Milne-Redhead (1985) 'In pursuit of the poplar', *Natural World* **10**, 26–28; H. L. Edlin, *What wood is that?*
27. J. Newsome (1964) *Pliny's Natural History*, Clarendon Press, Oxford.
28. J. Evelyn, *Sylva*; M. Agnoletti, pers. comm.
29. H. L. Edlin, *What wood is that?*; M. Eade, pers. comm.
30. R. Hall (1984) *The Viking Dig: Excavations at York*, The Bodley Head.
31. O. Rackham, *The History of the Countryside*.
32. M. Cook (1724) *Manners of Raising and Ordering Fruit Trees*.
33. R. Palmer (1992) *The Folklore of Herefordshire and Worcestershire*, Logaston Press.
34. H. L. Edlin, *What wood is that?*
35. C. Gardner, pers. comm.
36. P. Tabbush (1998) 'Genetic conservation of Black poplar (Populus nigra L.)', *Watsonia* **22**, 2, 173–179.
37. E. Milne-Redhead, 'In pursuit of the poplar'.
38. R. Harris, 'Poplar crucks in Worcestershire and Herefordshire'.
39. R. Harris, 'Poplar crucks in Worcestershire and Herefordshire'.
40. J. Costigan, S. Davies, C. Fogg, R. Harris and A. Hughes (1980) *Cholstrey Barn*, Avoncroft Museum of Buildings, Bromsgrove.
41. J. M. Paterson (1996) *Tree Wisdom*, Thorsons, London.
42. G. Grigson (1958) *An Englishman's Flora*, Helicon Publishing Ltd, Oxford.
43. D. Potterton (1983) *Culpeper's Colour Herbal*, W. Foulsham & Co. Ltd, Slough.
44. H. Friend (1884) *Flowers and Flower Lore*, W Swan Sonnenschein & Co, London.
45. E. Gutch and M. Peacock (1908) *Examples of printed folk-lore concerning Lincolnshire*, Folk Lore Society, London.
46. D. Potterton, *Culpeper's Colour Herbal*.
47. J. R. Watson (1987) *The Poetry of Gerard Manley Hopkins: A Critical Study*, Penguin Masterstudies, London.
48. J. D. Baird and C. Ryskamp (1995), *The Poems of William Cowper: Volume II 1782–1785*. Oxford, Oxford University Press.
49. J. M. Paterson, *Tree Wisdom*.
50. R. Graves (1948) *The White Goddess*, Faber & Faber, London.
51. R. D. Williams (1973) *The Aeneid of Virgil*, Macmillan Education Ltd, London.
52. R. Graves, *The White Goddess*.
53. R. Mabey, *Flora Britannica*.
54. H. Friend, *Flowers and Flower Lore*.
55. J. M. Paterson, *Tree Wisdom*.
56. R. Ceulemans, pers. comm.
57. H. Friend, *Flowers and Flower Lore*.
58. G. Grigson, *An Englishman's Flora*.
59. A. Morton (1996) *The Trees of Shropshire*. Airlife Publishing Ltd, Shrewsbury; J. E. Milner (1992) *The Tree Book*, Collins & Brown, London; R. Mabey, *Flora Britannica*.
60. J. White, pers. comm.
61. P. Hand, pers. comm.
62. B. J. Bailey (1981) *Portrait of Shropshire*, Robert Hale, London.
63. A. Morton, *The Trees of Shropshire*.
64. Hopesay Parish Council (1898) Minute Book.
65. Hopesay Parish Council (1898) Minute Book.
66. TC (1955) Untitled information leaflet produced by Tom Beardsley for Hopesay Parish Council; L. Player, J. Kirkpatrick, G. Messer, T. Beardsley *et al.* (1986) *200th Arbor Day Souvenir Booklet*; T. Beardsley (undated) *A few notes concerning the Arbor Tree*, Shropshire Archives no. TK17.2.
67. J. E. Auden (1912) Shropshire, Methuen & Co. Ltd, London.
68. C. Hole (1976) *British Folk Customs*, Hutchinson & Co, London.
69. B. J. Bailey, *Portrait of Shropshire*; C. Hole, *British Folk Customs*; L. Jones (1960) 'Letters to the Editor', *Folklore* **71**, 264–5.
70. C. Hole, *British Folk Customs*.
71. U. Rayska (1980) *The Arbor Tree – Aston on Clun. Shropshire*, eds V. M. E. Holt, A. H. Coles and D. G. Lloyd, Shropshire County Council, Shrewsbury.
72. R. Mabey and T. Evans (1981) *The Flowering Plants of Britain*, Hutchinson, London.
73. R. Mabey, *Flora Britannica*.
74. A. Morton, *The Trees of Shropshire*.

75. J. White, pers. comm.; P. Hand, pers. comm.; M. Jones, pers. comm.
76. Hopesay Parish Council (1959) Minute Book.
77. A. Morton, *The Trees of Shropshire.*
78. P. Hand, pers. comm.
79. J. Tsouvalis-Gerber (1997) *The social construction of nature: the case of forestry in Great Britain since the turn of the 20th century*, D. Phil. thesis, University of Oxford, Oxford.
80. C. Watkins (1998) *'A solemn and gloomy umbrage': changing interpretations of the ancient oaks of Sherwood Forest*, European Woods and Forests, Studies in Cultural History, CAB International.
81. http://www.geocities.com/CapitolHill/6142/hanging1.html (17 Feb 2004).
82. http://members.lycos.co.uk/WoodyPlantEcology/sycamore/lore.htm (17 Feb 2004).
83. D. Lloyd (1999) *The concise history of Ludlow*, Merlin Unwin Books, Ludlow.
84. H. T. Weyman (1913) *Ludlow in bye-gone days*, J. C. Austen & Son, Ludlow.
85. D. Lloyd, *The concise history of Ludlow.*
86. P. Hand, pers. comm.
87. W. Reynolds, pers. comm.
88. Anon. (2000) Summary Report for Area 20944, Gloucester Sites & Monument Record.
89. W. Reynolds, pers. comm.
90. Anon. (2000) Summary Report for Area 20944, Gloucester Sites & Monument Record.
91. S. Rudder (1779) *A new history of Gloucestershire*, Alan Sutton in collaboration with Gloucestershire County Library, Gloucester.
92. W. Watson, pers. comm.

Notes to Chapter Three: The Black Poplar in the Landscape

1. R. Bevan-Jones (2002) *The Ancient Yew*, Windgather Press, Macclesfield.
2. O. Rackham (1986) *The History of the Countryside*, Weidenfield & Nicholson, London.
3. F. M. R. Hughes, pers. comm.
4. G. Sharples, pers. comm.
5. O. Rackham, *The History of the Countryside.*
6. O. Rackham, *The History of the Countryside.*
7. J. Evelyn (1664) *Sylva: or a discourse on forest trees*, J. Martyn & J. Allesby, London.
8. O. Rackham, *The History of the Countryside.*
9. C. A. Stace (1971) 'The Manchester Poplar', *Watsonia* **8**, 391–3.
10. A. Mitchell and J. Wilkinson (1988) *Trees of Britain and Northern Europe*, Collins, London.
11. C. A. Stace, 'The Manchester Poplar'.
12. Anon. (1915) *Report on the City Parks and Recreation Grounds*, Manchester Parks Committee, Manchester.
13. J. Walsh, pers. comm.
14. Anon. (1915) *Report on the City Parks and Recreation Grounds.*
15. Anon. (1927–34) *Minutes of Parks and Cemeteries Committee of Manchester City Council*, Manchester City Council, Manchester.
16. J. Walsh, pers. comm.
17. Anon. (1927–34) *Minutes of Parks and Cemeteries Committee of Manchester City Council.*
18. A. Osborne (1933) *Shrubs and Trees for the Garden*, Ward, Lock & Co. Ltd, London.
19. Anon. (1899–1906) *Minutes of Parks and Cemeteries Committee of Manchester City Council*, Manchester City Council, Manchester.
20. Anon. (1899–1906) *Minutes of Parks and Cemeteries Committee of Manchester City Council.*
21. Anon. (1927–34) *Minutes of Parks and Cemeteries Committee of Manchester City Council.*
22. D. Rose, pers. comm.
23. J. Walsh, pers. comm.
24. J. Walsh, pers. comm.
25. J. Walsh, pers. comm.
26. R. Mabey (1996) *Flora Britannica*, Sinclair-Stevenson, London.
27. W. Page (1905–28) *The Victoria History of the County of Buckingham*, 4 vols, St Catherine Press, London.
28. H. L. Edlin (1969) *What wood is that?*, Thames & Hudson Ltd, Hertford.
29. R. Phillips, pers. comm.
30. W. Rose (1937) *The Village Carpenter*, Cambridge University Press, Cambridge.
31. M. Davies, pers. comm.
32. (http://www. nationmaster.com/encyclopedia/Buckinghamshire (4 July 2004).
33. R. Mabey, pers. comm.
34. R. Jefcoate, pers. comm.
35. A. Holmes, pers. comm.

Notes to Chapter Four: Black Poplar Population Surveys

1. E. Milne-Redhead (1990) 'The BSBI Black Poplar survey', *Watsonia* **18**, 1–5.
2. E. Milne-Redhead, 'The BSBI Black Poplar survey'.
3. E. D. Marquand (1901) *The Flora of Guernsey and the Lesser Channel Islands*, Dulau & Co, London.
4. R. Waterman, pers. comm.
5. J. A. Paton (1968) *Wild Flowers in Cornwall and the Isles of Scilly*, D. Bradford Books, Truro.
6. W. Keble-Martin (1939) *The Flora of Devon*, Buncle, Arbroath.
7. J. C. Mansell-Pleydell (1874) *The Flora of Dorsetshire*, Whittaker, London.
8. F. Townsend (1883) *The Flora of Hampshire*, Reeve, London.
9. E. M. R. Milne-Redhead (1975) 'Black Poplar Survey', *Watsonia* **10**, 295–6.
10. J. M. White (1972) *The Flora of Bristol*, Chatford House Press, Bristol.
11. D. Grose (1957) *The Flora of Wiltshire*, Wiltshire Archaeological & Natural History Society, Devizes.
12. H. J. Riddelsdell, G. W. Hedley and W. R. Price (1948) *The Flora of Gloucestershire*, Cotteswold Naturalist's Field Club, Cheltenham.
13. F. H. Arnold (1887) *The Flora of Sussex*, Hamilton, Adams & Co, London.
14. A. H. Wolley-Dod (1937) *The Flora of Sussex*, Kenneth Saville, Hastings.
15. F. J. Hanbury and E. S. Marshall (1899) *The Flora of Kent*, Hanbury, London.
16. C. E. Salmon (1931) *The Flora of Surrey*, G. Bell, London.
17. M. Cook (1724) *Manners of Raising and Ordering Fruit Trees.*
18. J. E. Little (1916) 'Hertfordshire Poplars', *Journal of Botany* **54**, 233–6.
19. H. Trimen (1869) *The Flora of Middlesex*, Robert Hardwicke, London.
20. D. H. Kent (1975) *The Historical Flora of Middlesex*, Ray Society, London.
21. G. C. Druce (1927) *The Flora of Oxfordshire*, Clarendon Press, Oxford.
22. G. C. Druce (1926) *The Flora of Buckinghamshire*, Buncle, Arbroath.
23. G. C. Druce (1930) *The Flora of Northamptonshire*, Buncle, Arbroath.
24. G. C. Druce (1927) *The Flora of Oxfordshire*, Clarendon Press, Oxford.
25. G. C. Druce (1930) *The Flora of Northamptonshire*, Buncle, Arbroath.
26. G. C. Druce (1926) *The Flora of Buckinghamshire*, Buncle, Arbroath.
27. M. Reed (1979) *The Buckinghamshire Landscape*, Hodder & Stoughton, London.
28. J. G. Dony (1953) *The Flora of Bedfordshire*, Corporation of Luton Museum and Art Gallery, Luton.
29. W. M. Hind (1889) *The Flora of Suffolk*, Gurney & Jackson, London.
30. F. Simpson (1982) *Flora of Suffolk*, Suffolk Naturalist's Society, Ipswich.
31. C. P. Petch and E. L. Swann (1968) *The Flora of Norfolk*, Jarrold & Sons, Norwich.
32. E. V. Rogers (1993) 'The native black poplar (Populus nigra subsp betulifolia) in Norfolk', *Transactions of the Norfolk Naturalists Society* **29**, 5, 375–82.
33. C. C. Babington (1870) *The Flora of Cambridgeshire*, McMillan & Bowes, Cambridge.
34. E. Lees (1867) *The Botany of Worcestershire*, Worcestershire Naturalists' Club, Worcester.
35. J. E. Bagnall (1891) *The Flora of Warwickshire*, Gurney & Jackson, London.
36. E. S. Edees (1972) *The Flora of Staffordshire*, David & Charles, Newton Abbot.
37. W. A. Leighton (1841) *A Flora of Shropshire*, John van Voorst, London.
38. C. A. Sinker, J. R. Packham, I. C. Trueman, P. H. Oswald, F. H. Perring and W. V. Prestwood (1985) *Ecological Flora of the Shropshire Region*, Shropshire Trust for Nature Conservation, Shrewsbury.
39. A. L. Primavesi and P. A. Evans (1988) *The Flora of Leicestershire.*
40. A. R. Hawood and C. W. F. Noel (1933) *The Flora of Leicestershire and Rutland*, Leicestershire Museums, Art Gallery and Records Service, Leicester.
41. G. Messenger (1971) *Flora of Rutland*, Leicestershire Museums, Leicester.
42. W. R. Linton (1903) *The Flora of Derbyshire*, Benrose & Sons Ltd, London.
43. A. R. Clapham (1969) *The Flora of Derbyshire*, County Borough of Derby Museum and Art Gallery, Derby.
44. G. Howitt (1839) *The Nottinghamshire Flora*, Hamilton, Adams & Co, London.
45. R. C. C. Howitt and B. M. Howitt (1963) *A Flora of Nottinghamshire*, private publication.
46. E. J. Gibbons (1975) *The Flora of Lincolnshire*, Lincolshire Naturalist's Union, Lincoln.
47. J. F. Robinson (1902) *The Flora of East Riding of Yorkshire*, A. Brown, London.

48. F. A. Lees (1898) *The Flora of West Yorkshire*, Reeve & Co, London.
49. N. Sykes (1993) *Wild Plants and Their Habitats in the North Yorkshire Moors*, North Yorkshire Moors National Park, York.
50. N. J. Winch and J. Thornhill (1807) *The botanist's guide through the counties of Northumberland and Durham*, J. Marshall, Gateshead upon Tyne.
51. G. A. Swan (1993) *Flora of Northumberland*, The Natural History Society of Northumbria, Newcastle on Tyne.
52. I. Lawrence (1994) *A Guide to the Wild Flowers of Cleveland*, Middlesborough County Council, Middlesborough.
53. G. G. Graham (1988) *The Flora and Vegetation of County Durham*, Durham Flora Committee and Durham County Conservation Trust, Durham.
54. W. G. Travis (1963) *Travis's Flora of South Lancashire*, Liverpool Botanical Society, Liverpool.
55. J. A. Wheldon and A. Wilson (1978) *The Flora of West Lancashire*, EP Publishing Ltd, Wakefield.
56. G. Halliday (1997) *A Flora of Cumbria*, University of Lancaster, Centre for North West Regional Studies, Lancaster.
57. R. G. Ellis (1993) *Aliens in the British Flora*, National Museum of Wales, Cardiff.
58. A. E. Wade, Q. O. N. Kay and R. G. Ellis (1994) *The Flora of Glamorgan*, HMSO, London.
59. H. A. Hyde and A. E. Wade (1957) *Welsh Flowering Plants*, National Museum of Wales, Cardiff.
60. D. A. Webb (1959) *An Irish Flora*, Dundalgan Press, Dundalk.
61. Anon. (1899) *Cybele Hibernica.*
62. D. D. Hobson (1991) *The black poplar in Ireland: its distribution and origin*, St John's College, The University of Oxford, Oxford.
63. P. Tabbush (1995) 'Native poplars and the restoration of floodplain forests', *Quarterly Journal of Forestry* **90**, 128–34; P. Tabbush (1998) 'Genetic conservation of Black poplar (Populus nigra L.)', *Watsonia* **22**, 173–9; E. V. Rogers (1995) 'The native black poplar (Populus nigra var. betulifolia (Pursh) Torr)', *Quarterly Journal of Forestry* **89**, 33–7.
64. R. Mabey (1996) *Flora Britannica*, Sinclair-Stevenson, London.
65. K. Pyne, pers. comm.
66. P. Jepson, pers. comm.
67. L. Starling, pers. comm.
68. M. O. Winfield, G. M. Arnold, F. Cooper, M. Le Ray, J. White, A. Karp and K. J. Edwards (1998) 'A study of genetic diversity in Populus nigra subsp. betulifolia in the Upper Severn area of the UK using AFLP markers', *Molecular Ecology* 7, 3–10.
69. M. Anderson, pers. comm.
70. F. Penfold, pers. comm.
71. K. J. Adams, pers. comm.
72. K. J. Adams, pers. comm.
73. L. Davies, pers. comm.
74. S. Falk, pers. comm.
75. P. Ennis, pers. comm.
76. M. Bagley, pers. comm.; F. Scire, pers. comm.
77. F. Wilmot, pers. comm.
78. E. Rogers, pers. comm.
79. N. Danby, pers. comm.
80. N. Danby, pers. comm.
81. L. Starling, pers. comm.
82. L. Weekes, pers. comm.
83. G. Easy, pers. comm.
84. D. Evans, pers. comm.
85. N. Lewis, pers. comm.
86. K. Pyne, pers. comm.
87. P. Jepson, pers. comm.
88. D. Green, pers. comm.
89. H. J. Elwes and A. Henry (1913) *The Trees of Great Britain and Ireland*, Edinburgh.
90. S. C. Holland (1992) *The Black Poplar in Gloucestershire*, FWAG, Gloucester.
91. C. Watkins, S. Holland and S. Thompson (1997) *A survey of black poplars (Populus nigra L.) in Herefordshire*, The University of Nottingham, Nottingham.
92. S. Bird, pers. comm.
93. F. Penfold, pers. comm.
94. C. Lowe, pers. comm.
95. I. C. Trueman, pers. comm.
96. J. White, pers. comm.
97. J. White, pers. comm.
98. O. Rackham (1986) *The History of the Countryside*, Weidenfield & Nicholson, London.
99. S. Robson, pers. comm.
100. E. Rogers, 'The native black poplar (Populus nigra var. betulifolia (Pursh) Torr)'.
101. O. Rackham (1995) *Trees and Woodlands in the British Landscape*, Weidenfield & Nicholson, London.
102. E. Milne-Redhead, 'The BSBI Black Poplar survey'.

Notes to Chapter Five: Genetic Analysis of the Black Poplar

1. A. H. D. Brown (1992) 'Human impact on plant gene pools and sampling for their conservation', *Oikos* **63**, 109–18.
2. J. E. J. White (1993) *Genetic Pollution of British Native Black Poplar, Populus nigra subsp betulifolia (Pursh) W. Wettst*, Symposium on Black Poplar, London, unpublished.
3. B. Heinze (1997) 'A PCR marker for a Populus deltoides allele and its use in studying introgression with native European Populus nigra', *Belgian Journal of Botany* **129**, 2, 123–30.
4. Anon. (1991) *Managing Global Genetic Resources: Forest Trees*, National Academy Press, Washington DC.
5. O. H. Frankel, A. H. D. Brown and J. J. Burden (1995) *The Conservation of Plant Biodiversity*, Cambridge University Press, Cambridge.
6. G. T. Prance (1997) 'The Conservation of Botanical Diversity' in *Plant Genetic Conservation: The In Situ Approach*, eds N. Maxted, B. V. Ford-Lloyd and J. G. Hawkes, Chapman & Hall, London, 3–14.
7. J. G. Hermsen (1989) 'Current use of potato collections' in *The Use of Plant Genetic Resources*, eds A. H. D. Brown, D. R. Marshall, O. H. Frankel and J. T. Williams, Cambridge University Press, Cambridge.
8. J. G. Hawkes (1970) 'Potatoes' in *Genetic Resources in Plants: Their exploration and conservation*, eds O. H. Frankel and E. Bennett, Blackwell Scientific Publications, Oxford.
9. O. H. Frankel *et al.*, *The Conservation of Plant Biodiversity.*
10. C. Keever (1953) 'Present composition of some stands of the former oak-chestnut forest in the southern Blue Ridge Mountains', *Ecology* 34, 44–54.
11. J. S. Boyce (1961) *Forest Pathology*, McGraw-Hill, New York.
12. J. L. Hamrick and M. J. W. Godt (1996) 'Conservation Genetics of Endemic Plant Species' in *Conservation Genetics: Case Histories from Nature*, eds J. C. Avise and J. L. Hamrick, Chapman & Hall, New York.
13. H. Huang, F. Dane and T. L. Kubisiak (1998) 'Allozyme and RAPD analysis of the genetic diversity and geographic variation in wild populations of the American chestnut (Fagaceae)', *American Journal of Botany* **85**, 7, 1013–21.
14. J. L. Hamrick and M. J. W. Godt, 'Conservation Genetics of Endemic Plant Species'.
15. K. E. Holsinger and L. D. Gottlieb (1991) 'Conservation of Rare and Endangered Plants: Principles and Prospects' in *Genetics and Conservation of Rare Plants*, eds D. A. Falk and K. E. Holsinger, Oxford University Press, Oxford.
16. W. J. Hahn and F. T. Grifo (1996) 'Molecular Markers in Plant Conservation Genetics' in *The Impact of Plant Molecular Genetics*, ed. B. W. S. Sobral, Birkhauser, Boston.
17. J. L. Hamrick and M. J. W. Godt, 'Conservation Genetics of Endemic Plant Species'.
18. G. M. Muluvi, J. I. Sprent, N. Soranzo, J. Provan, D. Odee, G. Flokard, J. W. McNicol and W. Powell (1999) 'Amplified fragment length polymorphism (AFLP) analysis of genetic variation in Moringa oleifera Lam.', *Molecular Ecology* **8**, 3, 463–70.
19. M. Rossetto, P. K. Weaver and K. W. Dixon (1995) 'Use of RAPD analysis in devising conservation strategies for the rare and endangered Grevillea scapigera (Proteaceae)', *Molecular Ecology* **4**, 321–9.
20. F. N. Wachira, R. Waugh, C. A. Hackett and W. Powell (1995) 'Detection of genetic diversity in tea (Camellia sinensis) using RAPD markers', *Genome* **38**, 201–10.
21. J. L. Hamrick and M. J. W. Godt, 'Conservation Genetics of Endemic Plant Species'.
22. S. Paul, F. N. Wachira, W. Powell and R. Waugh (1997) 'Diversity and genetic differentiation among populations of Indian and Kenyan tea (Camellia sinensis (L.) O. Kuntze) revealed by AFLP markers', *Theoretical and Applied Genetics* **94**, 255–63.
23. M. Byrne and G. F. Moran (1994) 'Population divergence in the chloroplast genome of Eucalyptus nitens', *Heredity* **73**, 18–28.
24. J. L. Hamrick, M. J. W. Godt and S. L. Sherman-Broyles (1992) 'Factors influencing levels of genetic diversity in woody plant species', *New Forests* **6**, 95–124.
25. M. J. W. Godt and J. L. Hamrick (1999) 'Population genetic analysis of Elliottia racemosa (Ericaceae), a rare Georgia shrub', *Molecular Ecology* **8**, 1, 75–82.
26. A. Angiolillo, M. Mencuccini and L. Baldoni (1999) 'Olive genetic diversity assessed using amplified fragment length polymorphisms', *Theoretical and Applied Genetics* **98**, 411–21.
27. T. Yamamoto, T. Shimada, K. Kotobuki, Y. Morimoto and M. Yoshida (1998) 'Genetic Characterisation of Asian Chestnut Varieties Assessed by AFLP', *Breeding Science* **48**, 4, 359–63.
28. L. Perera, J. R. Russell, J. Provan, J. W. McNicol and W. Powell (1998) 'Evaluating genetic relationships between indigenous coconut (Cocos nucifera L.)

accessions from Sri Lanka by means of AFLP profiling', *Theoretical and Applied Genetics* **96**, 545–50.
29. R. S. M. Drummond, D. J. Keeling, T. E. Richardson, R. C. Gardner and S. D. Wright (2000) 'Genetic analysis and conservation of 31 surviving individuals of a rare New Zealand tree, Metrosideros bartlettii (Myrtaceae)', *Molecular Ecology* **9**, 1149–57.
30. A. Legionnet and F. Lefevre (1996) 'Genetic variation of the riparian pioneer tree species Populus nigra L. I. Study of population structure based on isozymes', *Heredity* 77, 629–37.
31. A. Legionnet, P. Faivre-Rampant, M. Villar and F. Lefevre (1997) 'Sexual and asexual reproduction in natural stands of Populus nigra', *Botanica Acta* **110**, 3, 257–63.
32. B. Heinze (1997) 'A PCR marker for a Populus deltoides allele and its use in studying introgression with native European Populus nigra', *Belgian Journal of Botany* **129**, 2, 123–30.
33. P. Arens, H. Coops, J. Jansen and B. Vosman (1998) 'Molecular genetic analysis of black poplar (Populus nigra L.) along Dutch rivers', *Molecular Ecology* 7, 11–18.
34. J. van de Schoot, M. Pospiskova, B. Vosman and M. J. M. Smulders (2000) 'Development and characterisation of microsatellite markers in black poplar (Populus nigra L.)', *Theoretical and Applied Genetics* **101**, 317–22.
35. S. Bisoffi, pers. comm.
36. J. E. Cottrell, G. I. Forrest and I. M. S. White (1997) 'The use of RAPD analysis to study diversity in British black poplar (Populus nigra L. subsp. betulifolia (Pursh) W Wettst. (Salicaeae)) in Great Britain', *Watsonia* **21**, 305–12.
37. M. O. Winfield, G. M. Arnold, F. Cooper, M. Le Ray, J. White, A. Karp and K. J. Edwards (1998) 'A study of genetic diversity in Populus nigra subsp. betulifolia in the Upper Severn area of the UK using AFLP markers', *Molecular Ecology* 7, 3–10.
38. F. M. R. Hughes, N. Barsoum, K. S. Richards, M. Winfield and A. Hayes (2000) 'The response of male and female black poplar (Populus nigra L subspecies betulifolia (Pursh) W Wettst.) cuttings to different water table depths and sediment types: implications for flow management and river corridor biodiversity', *Hydrological Processes* **14**, 3075–98.
39. V. Storme, A. V. Broeck, B. Ivens, D. Halfmaerten, J. Van Slycken, S. Castiglione, F. Grassi, T. Fossati, J. E. Cottrell, H. E. Tabbener, F. Lefevre, C. Saintagne, S. Fluch, V. Krystufek, K. Burg, S. Bordacs, A. Borovics, K. Gebhardt, B. Vornam, A. Pohl, N. Alba, D. Agundez, C. Maestro, E. Notivol, J. Bovenschen, B. C. van Dam, J. van der Schoot, B. Vosman, W. Boerjan and M. J. M Smulders (2004) 'Ex-situ conservation of Black poplar in Europe: genetic diversity in nine gene bank collections and their value for nature development', *Theoretical and Applied Genetics* **108**, 6, 969–81.
40. J. E. Cottrell *et al.*, 'The use of RAPD analysis to study diversity in British black poplar (Populus nigra L. subsp. betulifolia (Pursh) W Wettst. (Salicaeae)) in Great Britain'.
41. M. O. Winfield *et al.*, 'A study of genetic diversity in Populus nigra subsp. betulifolia in the Upper Severn area of the UK using AFLP markers'.
42. F. Cooper, M. Jones, C. Watkins and Z. Wilson (2002) 'Genetic distribution and genetic diversity of black poplar.' Environment Agency Technical Report No. W1-O22.

Notes to Chapter Six: Conservation Strategies

1. www.alterra.nl/websites/europop/ (5 October 2001).
2. http://www-flobar.geog.cam.ac.uk/ (24 January 2003).
3. http://www.lhi.org.uk/projects_director y/projects_by_region/north_east/darlington/black_ poplar_project/poplar_editorial.html (24 January 2003).
4. http://www.nationalforest.org/fscene/s2003/water.html (24 January 2003).
5. P. Tabbush (1995) The status of black poplar conservation in Britain. Populus nigra Network. Casale Monferrato, Italy: IPGRI.
6. H. Gilbert-Carter (1932) *Our Catkin-Bearing Plants: An Introduction*, Oxford University Press, London.
7. M. Bonnet-Masimbert, pers. comm.
8. R. Mabey (1996) *Flora Britannica*, Sinclair-Stevenson, London.
9. J. White, pers. comm.
10. R. Southern, pers. comm.
11. F. M. P. Cooper (2001) *Geographic distribution and genetic diversity of black poplar*, Ph.D. thesis, School of Geography and School of Biological Sciences, The University of Nottingham, Nottingham.
12. J. E. Cottrell, G. I. Forrest and I. M. S. White (1997) 'The use of RAPD analysis to study diversity in British black poplar (Populus nigra L. subsp. betulifolia (Pursh) W Wettst. (Salicaeae)) in Great Britain', *Watsonia* **21**, 305–12; M. O. Winfield, G. M. Arnold, F. Cooper, M. Le Ray, J. White, A. Karp and K. J. Edwards (1998) 'A study of

genetic diversity in Populus nigra subsp. betulifolia in the Upper Severn area of the UK using AFLP markers', *Molecular Ecology* 7, 3–10.

13. E. M. R. Milne-Redhead (1985) 'In pursuit of the poplar', *Natural World* 10, 26–8.
14. J. White, pers. comm.
15. T. Green, pers. comm.
16. J. Evelyn (1664) *Sylva: or a discourse on forest trees,* J. Martyn & J. Allesby, London.
17. M. Cook (1724) *Manners of Raising and Ordering Fruit Trees.*
18. A. Holmes, pers. comm.
19. H. J. Elwes and A. Henry (1913) *The Trees of Great Britain and Ireland,* Edinburgh.
20. J. White (1993) *Black Poplar: the most endangered native timber tree in Britain,* Forestry Authority.
21. B. G. Bowes (1999) 'In vitro propagation from non-sterile explants' in *A Colour Atlas of Plant Propagation and Conservation,* ed. B. G. Bowes, Manson Publishing, London.
22. J. White, *Black Poplar: the most endangered native timber tree in Britain.*
23. J. White, pers. comm.
24. O. Rackham (1986) *The History of the Countryside,* Weidenfield & Nicholson, London.
25. P. Marren (1999) *Britain's Rare Flowers,* T. & A. D. Poyser Ltd, London.
26. S. Bird, pers. comm.; P. Ennis, pers. comm.

APPENDIX A

Identification Characteristics

Mature, standard specimens often lean heavily; they have an untidy appearance, with downsweeping lower branches and upsweeping upper branches. Pollards generally have a trunk some 2–3 m tall, the form and size of the crown being dependent upon when the tree was last pollarded. The bark is dark grey-brown (although colour varies geographically), deeply fissured and heavily bossed and burred (Figures 51 and 52) – although it should be noted that a bossless clone exists. Twigs are terete (cylindrical and tapering), have ascending tips, and often a yellow, viscous exudate. The current year's growth is pubescent, but this disappears in mid July and, occasionally, pubescent and glabrous twigs are present on the same tree. Buds have a ginger, shellac appearance and are outward-turning. Leaves are generally deltoid-ovate, but with great variation of size and shape, even on the same branch. During much of the year, they do not have leaf glands at the junction of lamina and petiole, but these may appear in late summer. Margins are serrated but not hooked, and are generally not ciliate (Figure 53). Petioles are laterally compressed and are pubescent. In spring, male catkins are crimson, female are lime green (Figures 54 and 55). Females produce copious amounts of fluffy seed in June (Figure 56). The presence of the aphid *Pemphigus populitransversus* may cause galls (spiral deformation) on some leaf petioles, but these are also found on the fastigiated forms of black poplar, and hybrids thereof. Suckers are not generally produced unless root damage has occurred, although root suckers have been seen on trees in the Vale of Aylesbury, usually after they have been pollarded. Native black poplar does not support mistletoe.

FIGURE 51.
Trunk of a black poplar, illustrating deeply fissured bark.
MARIANNE JONES

FIGURE 53.
Leaf from the Arbor Tree, illustrating the characteristic deltoid-ovate shape.
COURTESY OF ROSIE EVANS

FIGURE 52.
Burr on the trunk of a black poplar.
MARIANNE JONES

FIGURE 54.
Lime green female catkins.
JOHN WHITE, FORESTRY COMMISSION

FIGURE 55.
Crimson male catkins.
JOHN WHITE, FORESTRY COMMISSION

FIGURE 56.
Seed from black poplar with surrounding hydrophobic 'fluff'.
MARIANNE JONES

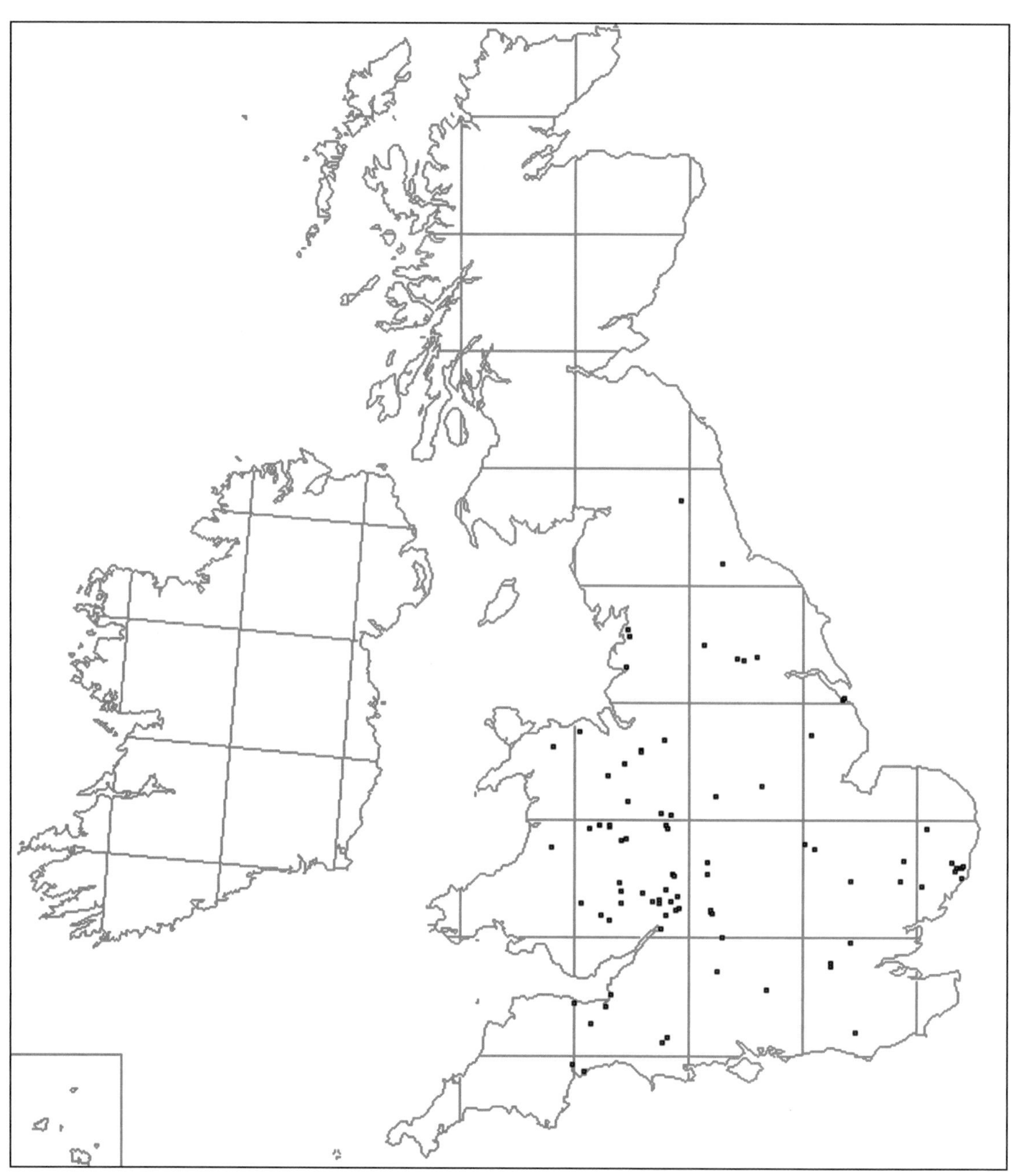

FIGURE 57.
Distribution map of notable trees that are worthy of a visit in England and Wales.
SCENESETTERS

APPENDIX B

Gazetteer of notable trees in Britain

For those readers who would like to go out and learn more about black poplar in the field, the list below details a number of notable trees throughout England and Wales, most of which are accessible, or at least visible, either by road or public footpath (and see Figure 57). There are many others, and enthusiasts will doubtless berate me for certain omissions, but I have a valid reason for this; it is that a visit requires landowner permission, and it is felt that too many visitors are undesirable; we do not want to turn landowners against their trees. The list includes a broad spectrum of the wide range of morphological types, along with pollards, standards, layering trees and those that are in picturesque settings. In addition to those trees listed, the Vale of Aylesbury and Greater Manchester populations are worthy of a visit, particularly the latter as it is unlikely to exist for many more years. Those trees listed in bold type are especially worth seeing, but please, once again, do not alienate landowners. The first digit of each co-ordinate relates to the Ordnance Survey tile reference, and is used in place of the prefix letters.

Key: M:male; F = female; NK = not known.

Grid Ref		*M*	*F*	*NK*	*Site*
2973	0914	1			Clyst St. Mary, flood plain R. Clyst
3077	**0852**	**1**			**Otterton, meadow by R. Otter**
3258	**1394**			**1**	**Cannington, by Cannington Brook**
3259	**1394**			**1**	**Cannington**
2990	1434	2			Dunster Deer Park, Pack Horse Bridge
3304	1499	1			Burnham-on-Sea
4233	**1698**	**1**			**Axford, R. Kennet**
3123	1262		1		Homington, trackside
3125	1262	2			Homington, riverside
3747	1088		2		Hazelbury Bryan
3798	1136		3		Fiddleford
4667	**1537**	**1**			**Basing, Pyotts Hill**
5441	1181		1		Isfield
5229	1740		1		Putney Heath, opposite Dover Park Road
5231	**1778**	**16**	**22**		**Barnes, Hammersmith Bridge**
5398	1943	1			Chingford, Epping Forest

Grid Ref		M	F	NK	Site
5830	2464	1			Foxearth, former mill
4268	1998		3		Grafton Lock, north of River Thames
6285	**2631**		**1**		**Framlingham, opposite Station Hotel**
6315	**2559**		**1**		**Campsea Ashe, west of Ashmoor Hall**
6321	2583		2		Marlesford
6367	**2581**		**1**		**Farnham, River Alde floodplain**
6376	**2501**	**1**			**Butley, near church**
6380	**2603**		**2**		**Benhall**
5858	2643		1		Bury St Edmunds, Abbey grounds
6025	2422	1			Hadleigh, near Toppesfield Bridge
6063	**2916**		**1**		**Old Buckenham**
5399	2471		1		Shepreth
5085	2742		1		Catworth, New Bridge, by stream
4990	**2787**	**1**			**Thrapston, by R. Nene**
3868	2222	5			Down Hatherley, golf course
3882	**2346**		**1**		**Mythe Fishing Lakes, Tewkesbury**
3902	**2238**	**1**			**Staverton, House In Tree Pub**
4178	2218		1		Wyck Rissington
4179	**2198**	**1**			**Bourton-on-the-Water, R. Dickler**
3667	2293	1			Kempley, north of Old Kempley Church
3721	**2285**	**1**			**Botloe's Green**
3721	2308	3			Ketford, Daffodil Bank
3742	**2068**	**1**			**Frampton on Severn, Berkeley Canal**
3788	2176	1			Apple Tree Inn, Minsterworth
3829	2303	1			Corse Lawn
3288	**2142**	**1**			**Abergavenny, Nevill Hall Hospital**
3369	2457	1			Duck Street, side lane by house
3387	**2287**	**1**			**Ewyas Harold**
3394	2384	3			Shenmore, by road junction
3581	2368	1			Mordiford
2782	**2762**	**1**			**Bewdley, bank of R. Severn**
3777	**2397**	**80**			**Castlemorton Common**
3835	**2523**	**1**			**Powick, traffic island**
3847	**2515**		**1**		**Powick Hams, by stream**
4148	**2532**			**1**	**Welford on Avon**
4149	2623		2		Wootton Wawen, by R. Alne
4208	**3192**		**1**		**Branston, by A38 and canal**
3269	3372	1			Bronygarth, by footpath
3392	**2818**	**1**			**Aston-on-Clun**
3433	**2836**	**1**			**Craven Arms, R. Onny footbridge**
3442	3153		1		Bicton, near Shrewsbury
3742	**3056**	**1**			**Evelith, flood plain Wesley Brook**
3783	2947	1			Hilton, bank of Hilton Brook

Grid Ref		*M*	*F*	*NK*	*Site*
3793	2921	1			Pondside, near Claverley
3831	3035	1			Hedgerow, east of Albrighton
3213	**2182**	**3**			**Crickhowell, R. Usk floodplain**
3043	**2283**	**1**			**Brecon**
3110	**2915**	**1**			**Newtown, car park**
3198	2953	1			Llandyssil, Cae Twm
3286	2937	1			Todlith Hill, Churchstoke
3295	2953	1			Roundton Hill House, Old Churchstoke
2796	3614			3	Llanwrst, flood plain
3418	**3463**			**1**	**Worthenbury, by Worthenbury Brook**
3035	3747			2	St. Asaph, R. Elwy
5048	**3720**		**2**		**Fiskerton churchyard**
5322	4016	2			Tetney
5340	4033	1			Tetney Lock
4627	**3278**	**3**	**2**		**Widmerpool, Fairham Brook**
3557	3563		1		Spurstow
3557	3585		2		Beeston
3569	3565	2	1		Spurstow
3761	**3665**	**1**			**Holmes Chapel, field by R. Croco**
3437	4290	1			Freckleton, garden boundary
3453	4615		1		Lancaster, Freeman's Wood
3459	4559	1			Conder Green, pub car park
4574	**4383**	**1**			**Cawood – Kelfield, by R. Ouse**
4116	4481	3			Ilkley, by R. Wharfe, river bank
4403	4367	1			Barwick in Elmet, by Longlane Beck
4466	**4354**	**4**	**1**		**Cold Hill, field near pond**
4271	**5183**		**1**		**Whessoe**
3917	5717	1			Humshaugh, by Humshaugh Burn

Index